Advance Praise for DOisms

AF207213

"Children are messages we send to a time we will never see. *DOisms* will help that message be more meaningful, emphatic, and lasting."
— Dr. David L. Long, Superintendent
Lake Elsinore Unified School District
Lake Elsinore, California

"If you are a parent, teacher, or young adult looking for creative, positive ways to bring out the best in children, *DOisms* will be especially valuable to you. The wisdom behind the ten DOisms will compel you to read with care so you can put into practice the advice offered by this sensitive and knowledgeable mother and teacher."
— Dr. Raymond J. Golarz and Marion J. Golarz
Educators, Educational Consultants, and Authors
Bloomington, Indiana

"*DOisms* is not so much about what children do as it is about what we do, and how we can alter our own behaviors to get the desired results. If we, as individuals, practice one DOism at a time, the experience of the kids we work and live with will be better."
— Dr. Katey Talbot, Director of Instructional Services
Lincoln Unified School District
Stockton, California

"Michelle Karns' love of children and faith in the goodness of people comes through on every page of this book. All adults will want to 'do' after reading this book about kids."
— Betty Herron, Executive Director
National Family Partnership of Arkansas
Little Rock, Arkansas

"The ten DOisms are very powerful and easy to implement. This great guide is a joy to read! To adults who say it's difficult to relate to today's youth, I say, 'Read DOisms!'"
— Robert C. Perkins, Superintendent
Twin Hills Union School District
Sebastopol, California

"In DOisms Michelle Karns has simplified many complex theories into very practical and DOable choices. Because of its child-centered foundation, this book is for all people who love children and who have a passionate commitment to the success of communities."
— Roberta Ellis, Chapter 1 Coordinator
Tulsa Public Schools
Tulsa, Oklahoma

"DOisms is must reading for those who want to love and understand adults and children, written by a woman who truly loves and understands us all."
— Rick Damelio, Superintendent
San Mateo–Foster City School District
San Mateo, California

DOisms

DOisms

Ten Prosocial Principles That Ensure Caring Connections with Kids

Michelle Karns

National Training Associates
Sebastopol, California

DOisms: Ten Prosocial Principles That Ensure
Caring Connections with Kids

Copyright © 1995 by National Training Associates
    First Printing June 1995
    Second Printing October 1997

Excerpt from *The Prophet* by Kahlil Gibran (page vii),
copyright © 1923 by Kahlil Gibran and renewed 1951 by
Administrators CTA of Kahlil Gibran Estate and Mary G.
Gibran. Reprinted by permission of Alfred A. Knopf, Inc.

Published by National Training Associates
P.O. Box 1270
Sebastopol, CA 95473
(800) 624-1120 PHONE
info@nta-yes.com EMAIL
www.nta-yes.com NTA ONLINE

Developmental Editor: Emily Garfield
Project Manager: Lorna Cunkle
Printer: Data Reproductions Corporation

ISBN 0-9636531-2-1

Your children are not your children.
They are the sons and daughters of Life's longing for itself.
They come through you but not from you.
And though they are with you yet they belong not to you.

You may give them your love but not your thoughts,
For they have their own thoughts.

You may house their bodies but not their souls,
For their souls dwell in the house of tomorrow, which you
cannot visit, not even in your dreams.

You may strive to be like them, but seek not to make them
like you.
For life goes not backward nor tarries with yesterday.

You are the bows from which your children as living
arrows are sent forth.
The archer sees the mark upon the path of the infinite, and
He bends you with His might that His arrows may go
swift and far.
Let your bending in the archer's hand be for gladness;
For even as He loves the arrow that flies, so He loves also
the bow that is stable.

— Kahlil Gibran (from *The Prophet*)

I dedicate this book to my husband, Robert, and our daughter, Katy. Robert makes it possible. Katy makes all the effort meaningful. They provide the impetus for my quest to better understand relationships and my passion to continue this life journey. My hope is that this book will lighten the load for all who share the adventure of loving and teaching children.

Contents

Foreword

This book is a philosophic reflection on ways for caring adults to interact more successfully with children, ways that enrich the quality of life for all. It is also a distillation of Michelle Karns' experiences with children and her observations of what has been effective for others.

What I particularly like about the book is that the guidelines suggested are succinct and, of course, eminently DOable. They lend themselves to becoming both a map for sequentially improving adult-child relationships and a checklist for achievement.

Michelle Karns writes for all adults who love kids, for all who are dedicated to preparing them for the future, and above all for those who fully understand the importance of intergenerational connections.

Welcome aboard.

— Emily Garfield, Ph.D.
Senior Staff Associate
National Training Associates

Preface

L ast year I was invited to address the International Committee for Drug Cessation at the United Nations. I recognized that I had been given a unique opportunity to reach policy makers, that what I had to say might conceivably change the lives of a number of people I would never see. This forced me to reexamine my ideas and beliefs, review my life work, analyze my choice of direction, and reaffirm my course of action. This book is the result of that inquiry.

Instead of focusing on what is wrong with kids and how risky it can be to work with them, I organized my thoughts in terms of what we can actually DO. I am distressed at how much energy is spent talking about how bad things are. I am tired of the endless media coverage of the day's horrors. Everything seems to have a negative twist to it. Rather than presuming a problem, I am committed to making a positive, front-end difference. This shift in my thinking has affected my own life, how I view my work, and what I want to DO.

My daughter Katy's first day of kindergarten was tough. A boy she didn't know punched her in the eye. No provocation, no prior history, nothing. He hit my kid! She came home and reported her dilemma and announced that she would not go back to school until he was gone. No amount of rational discussion worked. She went to bed in tears, woke up in tears, and tearfully was walked to school.

The first semester was fraught with stories of "torture." (She sometimes exaggerates but the teacher confirmed that she was into a fatal attraction. She also confirmed that this boy was a "special needs" kid.) When it came time to plan Katy's birthday party, she said she wanted to invite the awful child. I asked "Why?" She quickly retorted, "Because nobody else will invite him to a party. He must be lonely."

He was invited but was unable to attend, and so the story goes, until the last week of school when the awful child almost punched her again. This time she said, "Please don't hit me" — and he didn't! As she told me how she handled the most recent incident, she matter-of-factly explained, "Mom, some kids are born different." When I asked how she knew this, she was quick to answer, "I figured it out by myself."

I like to think that Katy shifted her perspective. Instead of holding on to the negative, she consciously chose to turn around the "torture" and create a new truth. Her response was far more mature than mine. Is your orientation focused upon the problem or the solution? Check yourself.

Birthing a baby and striving to be a good parent. Being a colleague and a friend. Creating classrooms that are fun and worthy of a child's attention. All of my roles have prepared me to write *DOisms*. Kids are the center of my life experiences. I have always worked with children in some capacity. I have been a counselor, a teacher, a family guide, and a trainer. In all these roles, I have come to value the experience of children and to truly understand the necessity of childhood. Every day provides a new opportunity for me to discover truths about kids and their current reality. I understand that effective relationships with children meet them inside this reality. This understanding has helped me frame what caring adults must DO with kids.

I once saw a T-shirt that proclaimed, "It is never too late to have a childhood." I couldn't fully fathom what this meant until the birth of my own daughter. I am fully committed to providing her with childhood experiences that will support her for a lifetime. I have come to recognize that childhood is about learning to survive for the future. When I spoke at the United Nations, I wove into my comments my strong belief that every child needs adults to nurture, guide, and support their development.

The United Nations presentation started a process. This book completes the cycle. *DOisms* reflects my new way of thinking and provides a roadmap of what is necessary to serve kids of the next generation. Throughout the book I have utilized the words of many significant thinkers and DOers. I am grateful to them; they have helped me think and DO differently. I now pass the baton on to you.

— Michelle Karns
March 1995
Davis, California

Acknowledgments

I am forever grateful to the many people who helped me write what I wanted to say and felt was needed. It is always special when I am confronted with the fact that many others think and feel as I do. While I have dedicated this book to my family and the children I serve, I want to thank some folks who may not even know how much they have contributed to making this a reality.

> I appreciate and value the team of women who took the time to read these words, give feedback, and support me: Susan, Katy, Lou, and Emily.

> I am forever grateful for the ever-present support from Wayne Hunnicutt and Nancy Scott. I am committed to the process I share with Kitty.

> I am in awe of Stephen Covey, whose masterful words of wisdom always seem to border on the spiritual. I value his ability to share his truths.

> Thanks to my mom I have a love of words, and from my dad I received the gift of laughter.

These thanks are very important to me. I am blessed with people who care and have hope for all the children. We will make a difference if we stay close to our hearts.

The Basic Assumptions

If you want to live a long life,
focus on making contributions.
— Hans Selye[1]

ADOism is a positive, prosocial action that can enhance the quality of your relationships. Two critical ingredients — courage and a belief in the human spirit — frame the DOisms. Together they culminate into strategies that make your connections with children more helpful and meaningful. The DOisms are intended to serve you in this moment and your children in their future.

The DOisms can help you stay focused on what you can DO *now* to enrich your relationships with children. They can help you frame the children's lives in terms of opportunity and hope rather than despair and failure. Remember the challenge of Robert F. Kennedy:

Few will have greatness to bend history itself, but each of us
can work to change a small portion of events....it is from
numberless acts of courage and belief that human history is
shaped.[2]

Each of the ten DOisms leads to a single, ultimate purpose: the building of a caring child-supporting community. The best way to support all children is by creating systems of people who care. Caring is an act between two people. Only with another human can caring be experienced and reciprocated. You know that caring is happening when you become conscious of desiring positive outcomes and become invested in the success of someone else. Caring is evident when you place value on your relationships and behave in ways that honor your relationships. A community that cares will invest in its youth, value differences, prepare for the future, and strive to improve the quality of life for all its members.

Used well, the DOisms can strengthen the connections that give relationships their value and worth. They are designed to promote prosocial interactions with children. Why are prosocial skills so important? They are the foundation of good relationships, shared positive experiences, and healthy expectations. A prosocial dynamic makes you smile when you see a smile, makes you laugh when you hear laughter, and helps your tears fall when you encounter tragedy. You are being prosocial when you express gratitude, kindness, and generosity without creating obligations. Prosocial civility prevents us from stealing others possessions and hurting each other. A prosocial exchange occurs when people compromise, collaborate, and cooperate. The ultimate goal of the prosocial dynamic is to improve life's circumstances, enhance life's adventures, and discover life's meaning.

Connecting with others provides a powerful life force. Working together and savoring the resulting richness is the greatest of all gifts. The most dynamic rationale for joining together with others is the commonly held belief that together we can do what none of us can do alone. The more effort we put into helping people connect, the better off we'll all be.

> *Every thing and everybody is connected. Everything affects every thing else. No matter how different, no matter how far away, we are all part of an interconnected whole.*
> — George Land and Beth Jarman[3]

> *Kindness is the key to changing the violent nature of today.*
> — Dr. Benjamin Spock[4]

The dominant principle of social life is not the struggle for existence, but cooperation.... If we would seek for one word that describes society better than any other, the word is cooperation.
— Ashley Montagu[5]

Each of these statements reflects a belief in the ability of people, in change, and in the processes that people share. The ultimate challenge for any of us living in these turbulent times is to live as we want our children to live. As adults we must realize that the way we treat children will be the basis upon which we are judged as a generation. I desperately want to DO well for my daughter and all of the children I serve, but I can't DO it alone. For the purpose of calling adults to attention, I have narrated what I hope will contribute to your decision to join forces for the sake of our children.

LET'S START WITH THE FIVE basic assumptions about kids that provide the structure upon which to build quality relationships. Acceptance of these assumptions will help you strategize how to approach and develop connections with children.

1. All kids need adults who don't shame and blame them.

While trying to figure out how to describe a healthy relationship, I realized that real nurturing and caring can only be expressed without shame and blame. To develop environments that do not utilize shame and blame, adults need to set clear and sensible rules and manage conflict well. Healthy expectations, meaningful work, and hope for the future are also essential. When shame and blame, unresolved conflict, and uncertainty are present, every interaction awaits the dropping of the proverbial other shoe. Children who learn to expect the negative seem tainted by every experience, and then they perpetuate the cycle. Negative fosters negativity. Let go of shame and blame, and your relationships with children will become more rewarding for both of you.

2. All kids behave in ways that benefit them.

Rudolf Dreikurs, author of *Children: The Challenge,* proposes that we look for the benefit the child perceives in the behavior we are witnessing. He offers a checklist of common misbehaviors and the likely benefit.[6]

If the child:	The benefit is likely:
Annoys you	Attention
Angers you	Power
Hurts you	Revenge
Makes you despair	Assumed inadequacy

Understanding this dynamic has helped me discern the possible benefit of the behaviors that I observe. Intervention occurs when I attempt to replicate the benefit of the behavior in socially appropriate terms. Here are some possible prosocial interventions for each behavioral benefit.

Attention

Provide options for new responsibilities.

Participate in a new and difficult activity with the child.

Assign a role in the school play.

Ask the child to participate in special training as a helper.

Have the student work with you in the classroom.

Let the child work with others.

Power

Give the child a title.

Ask the child to help.

Ask the child's opinion and acknowledge its value.

Let the child lead.

Engage the child with other adults.

Revenge

Read about bullies.

Create stories and role plays that allow people to be angry.

Validate that anger is acceptable.

Use literature and history to start dialogues about rage.

Use TV news to give assignments regarding violence.

Talk openly about feelings.

Despair

Speak clearly about your feelings.

Voice your questions about why this is happening:
"I really don't understand what's going on. I can only
guess that...."

Write a letter.

Make a book of pictures that reflects the positive and
"good" times.

Tell the child that you'll be okay and that you hope the
child will be okay, too.

To become a master at using this technique, you have to accept that the benefit of behavior may not be logical, rational,
or make sense to you. Furthermore, the benefit may not be
part of the child's consciousness; that is, the child is not

always able to understand why he behaves the way he does. The well-known answer "I don't know" is often the truth!

3. All kids need to feel competent.

A few years ago there was a concerted effort to raise kids' self-esteem. While the idea was a good one, many program providers found uniform achievement difficult. I remember one teacher who told me he had a wonderful self-esteem strategy and then pulled out a variety of imprinted stickers. I often joke about this teacher, who apparently thinks that the lack of self-esteem is a sticker deficiency.

I didn't understand at the time what was wrong with this popular approach, I just knew it was off the mark. Too many kids were being left out of the cycle of support — stickerless, if you will. Subsequently, I started to tap into the resiliency research, which highlights competence as the trait that enables at-risk children to survive adversity. Norman Garmezy, a resiliency research pioneer, introduced the concept of competence in a manner that is easily understood. He states, "Competence is the ability to interact effectively with the environment and the ability to be flexible in the environment."[7] Garmezy goes on to maintain that certain characteristics provide evidence of competence: healthy expectancies, personal worthiness, self-discipline, critical and reflective thinking, friendships, and future-orientation with the ability to delay gratification.

The more I studied, the clearer it became that competence — not rewards, applause, or support — is the root of self-esteem. As a result, building competence through real, meaningful work and productive, creative learning has become the foundation of my work with children.

4. All kids need guidance, values, and an internal dialogue to support prosocial behavior.

As growing numbers of kids lack the positive adult role models that are needed to establish life values, we see more kids operating from negative beliefs. In this negative kids' world, it is far too acceptable to be bad and too few children seem to desire excellence through a positive, sustained effort. Emile Durkheim, the noted French sociologist, aptly described our current situation when he said, "When morés are sufficient, laws are unnecessary. When morés are insufficient, laws are unenforceable."[8]

The thrust of our efforts with children must support a prosocial orientation with self-regulation as a vital aspect of development. When values are internalized, a personal kind of self-talk develops and becomes what is known as the "internal locus of control."[9] Jean Piaget agrees: "Rules imposed by external constraint remain external to the child's spirit. Rules due to mutual respect and cooperation take root in the child's mind."[10]

For rules to be unnecessary, self-discipline must be developed in our children. Coupled with delayed gratification, self-discipline will provide kids with the internal dialogue that supports a positive social orientation. Stephen Covey, an organization specialist, would agree with this approach. He claims that you don't empower others if you have to control them.[11]

5. All kids need laughter, friendship, and physical challenges.

My personal experiences with kids are most successful when I focus on the process rather than the outcome. Laughter, play, and appropriate physical challenges foster great relationships that offset the need many kids seem to have to engage in potentially self-destructive behaviors. A good belly laugh can duplicate many illicit highs and physical exercise can boost the morale. When fun and play are a part of your everyday activities, children will stay hooked into the relationship. Build a relationship and good lives follow.

FROM THESE FIVE ASSUMPTIONS, I have distilled a set of beliefs that serve as my operating truths when I parent and work with children.

- All children need nurturing and positive relationships with adults.

- Adults need to take the time to figure out why a child chooses a specific behavior. It is our responsibility as adults to meet children in *their* reality.

- Self-esteem is a product of experiences and opportunities that foster competency. Competence is best supported through cooperation, not competition.

- All children need a positive social orientation based on an acceptance of rules that have been internalized and valued. This prosocial orientation makes safety, respect, and hopefulness possible.

- Humor, spontaneous play, physical movement, and a positive attitude provide the basis for a quality relationship with children.

Note the similarities between the assumptions and the beliefs; they should be congruent. Together these assumptions and beliefs frame my behavior and attitudes.

I BELIEVE OUR COMMITMENT to kids will make a difference. Adults are needed who have the passion and desire to meet kids in their reality and who don't make excuses for their part in kids' failures. The roles adults play in kids' lives are not as important as their commitment. Kenneth Blanchard says it best: "There's a difference between interest and commitment. When you're interested in doing something, you do it only when it is convenient. When you're committed to something, you accept no excuses, only results."[12]

The DOisms provide the treatise for participation in this movement toward commitment. If you love kids, if you'll take the time to listen to them, and if you enjoy the laughter that erupts from the belly, you can belong. To paraphrase the words of Rosa Parks, the civil rights pioneer, get disenchanted and DO something differently.[13]

I think the world is a dance floor, not a stage. We choose how we dance through our lives. The steps we take, the pace we set, the rhythm we hear, and how we flow with our partners are all products of our personal realities filtered through perceptions and experience. How do *you* dance with children?

Notes

1. Hans Selye, quoted in *Quotes and Quips* (Provo, UT: Covey Leadership Center, 1993), p. 50.

2. Robert F. Kennedy, quoted in *Even Eagles Need a Push: Learning to Soar in a Changing World* by David McNally (New York: Delacorte, 1990), p. 38.

3. George Land and Beth Jarman Land, *Break-point and Beyond: Mastering the Future* (New York: HarperBusiness, 1992).

4. Benjamin Spock, *Today Show,* September 1994. See also *A Better World for Our Children: Rebuilding American Family Values* by Benjamin Spock (Bethesda, MD: National Press Books, 1994).

5. Ashley Montagu, quoted in *Tribes: A New Way of Learning Together* by Jeanne Gibbs (Santa Rosa, CA: Center Source Publications, 1994), p. 37.

6. Rudolf Dreikurs and Lawrence Zuckerman, *Children: The Challenge* (New York: NAL-Dutton, 1991).Other excellent sources for information about effective remedies for the four mistaken goals of behavior include the following:
H. Stephen Glenn and Jane Nelsen, *Positive Discipline A–Z* (Rocklin, CA: Prima, 1993).
Don Dinkmeyer and Gary D. McKay, *The Parent's Handbook: Systematic Training for Effective Parenting* (New York: Random, 1989).
Don Dinkmeyer and Gary D. McKay, *Parenting Teenagers: Systematic Training for Effective Parenting* (New York: Random, 1990).

7. Norman Garmezy and Michael Rutter, *Stress, Coping and Development in Children* (Baltimore: Johns Hopkins University Press, 1984).

8. Emile Durkheim, quoted in *Quotes and Quips* (Provo, UT: Covey Leadership Center, 1993), p. 54.

9. Julian B. Rotter, *Social Learning and Critical Psychology* (Englewood Cliffs, NJ: Prentice-Hall, 1954).

10. Jean Piaget, *The Moral Judgment of the Child* (New York: Free Press, 1965), p. 366.

11. Stephen Covey, *Principle-Centered Leadership: Strategies for Personal and Professional Effectiveness* (New York: Simon & Schuster, 1992).

12. Kenneth Blanchard, quoted in *Even Eagles Need a Push: Learning to Soar in a Changing World* by David McNally (New York: Delacorte, 1990), p. 151.

13. Rosa Parks told a reporter, "I knew someone had to take the first step." For her, the first step came on December 1, 1955, in Montgomery, Alabama, when she refused to give up her seat to a white person. See *Rosa Parks: The Movement Organizes* by Kai Friese (Englewood Cliffs, NJ: Silver Burdett Press, 1990).

Sort to the Positive

No problem can be solved
from the same consciousness that created it.
— Albert Einstein[1]

Physicist Albert Einstein proposed that an effective solution comes only with a change in perspective and perception. When you are stuck, solutioning always requires a shift in perception. This shift is within each person's control and is always an aspect of choice. We are in control of our lives and we demonstrate personal power by remaining conscious of what we choose to believe, how we behave, and how we cast ourselves into the future.

In *What to Say When You Talk to Your Self,* Shad Helmstetter examines the negative programming that pervades our society. "Leading behavioral researchers have told us that as much as seventy-seven percent of everything we think is negative, counterproductive, and works against us," he writes.[2] But because we are in charge of our own perceptions, each of us can make choices that will help us stay focused on the positive.

Noticing what works in a given situation rather than what is not working is sorting to the positive. Someone who sorts negatively looks at what is wrong, seeks someone or something to blame, rates situations in terms of how bad they are, and sees challenges as constraints. Someone who sorts to the positive looks at what can be done to better achieve goals, sees challenges as opportunities, takes responsibility, and is driven by hope and a desire to self-improve.

For many, the natural sort — a first response based on how experiences are ordered and classified — is to the negative. Too many people are conditioned to view their experiences in terms of what is not, rather than what is or could be. Those who tend to sort to the negative seem caught in a cycle of nay-saying and reliving tough times. They can be heard saying things like "It must be my fault," "I wonder what I did to deserve this," and "Why me?"

Some people are forever hoping that the natural consequences of a given circumstance will not occur. Morning won't follow night. Five o'clock traffic will not slow me down. I will wake up and not have to go to work. This becomes a negative sort when natural consequences are viewed as a personal affront, happening only to me, while everyone else has a better life. The negative sort becomes a negative reality through which the world is viewed.

Shaming, blaming, wishing things are not as they are — these are all descriptive of a negative sort, a negative reality, as is the far too familiar "Not good enough." Shame and blame eventually lead to alibis and excuses. The negative sort is cyclic and pervasive, and kids on the receiving end tend to become negative and hopeless. They tend to feel that their accomplishments are valued by what they should have done rather than what they did accomplish. I am reminded of the many children who bemoan that no matter how well they do, their parents want more. "If I get a B, my parents want an A. If I get an A, they want straight A's."

The shame-and-blame phenomenon can also be seen every time children say to themselves, "If only I had worked harder," "If only I had not forgotten…," or "If only I had been given better parents…." Shame and blame are at the root of most childhood anguish. And many adults never shed their childhood shame and blame, thereby passing the disaster on to their children.

Perhaps you suffer from this malady. Is your orientation focused on the problem or the solution? Answer the following questions to find out.

1. When things go wrong, is it always someone else's fault?
2. Do you consider yourself a victim of circumstances?
3. Do you assume responsibility for things that are not under your control?
4. Do you judge your insides by others' outsides?
5. Do you harbor resentments against people who seem to have an easier life than you?

A "yes" to any of these questions indicates that you have become vulnerable to negativity. This is not a scientific test. It is comprised of conditions that I have noted anecdotally about folks who get stuck in negativity.

A negative sort always seems to have at least two of the following characteristics:

Shame
I stole from my mom. She says she forgives me, but I know she doesn't. I never do the right things.

Blame
If she hadn't come to the party, I wouldn't have gotten drunk. She's the problem.

Inaccurate assumption of responsibility
I caused my parents' divorce.

Self-degradation
I can't do anything right.

Faulty comparisons
I will never be as good as Sheila. She doesn't even try and
she gets good grades.

Our society seems to be populated with an ever-increas-
ing number of chronic shamers and blamers. Too many people are focused on what is wrong. Read a newspaper. Watch
the news. Everything contributes to a negative sort, right?

If you agree, you have allowed me to lead you down a
negative path. We've *allowed* outside forces to determine our
reality. Members of the mass media have power because we
give them power, which has resulted in a corresponding loss
of personal power. We have the ability to lessen the effect of
outside forces, but to do so requires that we change how we
currently behave.

We are in charge by choice, not by chance. We can choose
to be creative and positive, rather than reactive and negative.
Ed Oakley and Doug Krug, in *Enlightened Leadership,* classify
people who have these two opposing perspectives — sorting
to the negative versus sorting to the positive — as reactive
(negative) thinkers and creative (positive) thinkers.[3] Table 1.1
outlines these two extremes (see page 15).

Oakley and Krug have succinctly summarized a lifetime
of my own observations. By describing the behaviors that are
most often observed, they take the comparison out of the
realm of a value judgment. They further delineate the positive
and negative by assigning common traits to each orientation.
Again, they seem to hit the target.

Table 1.2 underscores why the positive-solution orientation is so vital (see page 16). It is the only way to *move* toward
something new. The negative focus sustains the reactive past,
where little is new or creative. Shifting from embellishing
the old to creating the new is a major thrust of sorting to the

Table 1.1 Extreme Thinking Styles[4]

Reactive Thinkers	Creative Thinkers
Are resistant to change.	Are open to change.
See reasons they *cannot* do things.	Are "can do" oriented.
Focus on finding problems to fix.	Build on successes and strengths.
Are blinded by problems in a situation.	Seek the opportunity in every situation.
Avoid blame or responsibility.	Take responsibility for their actions.
Are limited by what worked in the past.	Think in terms of new possibilities.
Are poor listeners.	Are good listeners.
Run out of energy quickly.	Have a continuous supply of energy.
Find it difficult to choose and decide.	Make choices and decisions easily.
Feel they have no control of their environment.	Feel in control of their environment.
Often work very hard.	Get results without trying hard.
Are afraid of risks or major challenges.	Are driven to excel by challenge/risk.
Suffer excessive inner stress.	Enjoy an inner calmness.
Cannot let go of the past.	Are current and future oriented.
Have low self-esteem.	Have high self-esteem.
Are devastated by failure.	Learn and grow from their mistakes.
Focus on what they want to avoid.	Focus on results they want.
Do things right.	Do the right things.

Table 1.2 Problem Versus Solution Orientation[5]

A Problem Orientation

Puts a spotlight on what is not working.

Looks for someone to blame.

Causes defensiveness.

Stifles creativity.

Causes more problems as attention is drawn to the problems that already exist.

Drains off valuable energy.

Keeps us stuck in boxes.

A Solution Orientation

Puts a spotlight on strengthening what is already working.

Develops openness and involvement.

Naturally moves us toward the goal it is focused upon.

Creates energy and enthusiasm.

Creates open communication and continuous renewal.

Develops the atmosphere best suited for generating creative solutions.

positive. In a similar manner, George Bernard Shaw challenges us to take charge. While his words don't say, "You create your world," I think that was his intent.

> *People are always blaming their circumstances for what they are. I don't believe in circumstances. The people who get on in this world are the people who get up and look for the circumstances they want, and, if they can't find them, make them.*[6]

Who is in charge of how you focus your energy? Your peers? The media? Your elders? The answer is simple: whoever or whatever you choose. You control your perceptions. You construct the paradigms and personal filters that govern how you respond to the experiences of your daily life. Three separate dimensions must be aligned to create an opportunity to sort to the positive.

Perceptions: how we see the world

Paradigms: the philosophical framework or model that dictates how we *should* behave

Personal filters: how we interpret our experiences

Our perceptions create our reality. Our paradigms frame our behavior. Our personal filters give meaning to our experiences. Alignment occurs when the three dimensions agree. People who have one element out of alignment with the other two will find their life experiences difficult to manage. The result of this misalignment is stress.

The challenge is to create alignment and reduce stress through self-reflection. Learn to ask these basic questions:

What is my perspective in this situation?

What are my expectations?

What would I like to change about the circumstances?

What do I know or believe about the situation?

What would be the most useful course of action?

Answering these questions will help you decide which of the three dimensions might be out of alignment. Then ask yourself questions about the cause of the misalignment:

Is it what I believe?

Is it how I perceive?

Is it how I behave?

Is it a problem with my expectations?

You can use this approach with children by changing the questions but sticking with the intent of each component. For example, ask any of the following:

Perceptions

How did you choose to do this?

What are you thinking?

How did you think this up?

Did you think this up yourself?

Paradigms

Do you think that is the right thing to do?

Who else does it that way?

Would your parents agree to this?

Help me understand why you think this is right.

Personal filters

Is that what you thought would happen?

Did you expect this?

How did you know this would happen?

Were you surprised?

Learning how to ask appropriate questions is critical to helping children view current reality in terms that will be positive and prosocial. Most children willingly embrace such a response. They strive to do well, be well, and think well of others. Since they are naturally attracted to the polarities of good and bad, sorting to the positive is attractive to them.

I can think of only one means to this positive end: Change how we think, how we view our world, and what we do with one another. Adults must take the time to create the conditions that focus on the positive. This is a vital part of teaching children to be creative. The nine steps to positive sorting should help.

Nine Steps to Positive Sorting

1. Start with a positive attitude.

Having a positive attitude does not mean that you gleefully walk through life, ignoring everything negative. In *Even Eagles Need a Push*, David McNally describes the positive thinker.

> *A positive attitude does not dissolve life's problems; rather, it is an effective constructive approach to dealing with them. The positive thinker accepts life as it unfolds without trying to control it or have it conform to limited human expectations. The positive thinker regards life as an adventure where the rewards are in the risks and the pleasure in responding to the challenge.*[7]

McNally highlights two important aspects of developing a positive attitude: letting go and becoming responsive. It is not coincidental that in a growing body of research analyzing those who survive gross and chronic adversity, resilient children stand out as having a positive attitude, a future-focused orientation, and an understanding that personal choice frames all behavior.

For DOism 1 to be valid, a positive attitude is not enough. The intentions must be clear and the presentation must be congruent with the words chosen. I'll never forget Daniel, a teen I counseled whose father wanted excellence. Daniel was a straight A student, an active and positive role model, and a hard worker. When he was not accepted to his father's Ivy League alma mater, the parental response was: "We love him anyway." The words were positive but the hidden message was negative.

2. Be positive in your role modeling.

As an adult in a child's life, you can model whatever it is that you expect, for what you model is always what you will get back. If you want polite behavior, model it and reinforce it. If you want clean rooms, model it and reinforce it. If you want generosity and kindness of spirit, model it and model it again.

Adults have the opportunity to help children develop their abilities and perspectives. Kids can *see* their image as "good" if the mirror is held by someone they trust, especially if that person *does* "good" as well! Somehow, those who serve as guides and mentors must reconnect our children to what *can be* instead of burdening them with all that has gone wrong. Our kids need us to sort to the positive, to guide and serve others, and to contribute to the well-being of all of us.

Whenever there is a lack of clarity, children will be left to the devices of their peers. When children rely on peers as re-sources to manage life's happenstances, they miss opportuni-ties for personal growth. Instead of learning to make choices, they fall into the trap of doing what others have done. Too often peer-led realities define adults as the enemy. When adults become the enemy, children lose their experienced mentors and guides.

3. Operate from a consistent mind-set.

Our choices construct the filters through which we view the world. Much like the lens on a camera, our mind-set helps us discern and respond to the reality that is uniquely ours.

An example: You are watching a TV rerun of *Leave It to Beaver*. You decide to switch to the new *Star Trek*. Once you change the channel, you think differently, you perceive the world in new terms, and you have different expectations for behavior. If Beaver asked to be beamed up, you would note a gross discrepancy in the story line. If Captain Kirk sought advice from Ward Cleaver, you would think he had lost his place in time.

Incongruency causes confusion. Managing the current reality becomes difficult. Much of the difficulty we experience in living with children is a product of incongruity. I know this occurs because so many kids are tuned out and angry. They have difficulty determining what is real in their lives. Incongruity creates a double bind, a lose-lose. "I can't win here" is a common call from children attempting to make sense out of non-sense.

4. Stay conscious and in control of how you behave.

I am increasingly convinced that large segments of our society are committed to unconsciousness. How do I know this? Conscious people wouldn't allow children to go hungry. They wouldn't allow violence, retribution, and hatred. Conscious people wouldn't allow racist acts. They wouldn't allow the judicial system to erode or democracy to be threatened.

Warren Bennis and Joan Goldsmith describe the difference between ethics, consciousness, and behavior as an "integrity gap."[8] Consistency between all variables of identity are vital to self-expression. Beliefs, attitudes, behavior, and relationships must be congruent. Dr. Martin Luther King addressed this issue from a Birmingham jail:

> *I am coming to feel that the people of ill will have used time*
> *much more effectively than the people of good will. We will have*
> *to repent in this generation not merely for the vitriolic works*
> *and actions of bad people, but for the appalling silence of the*

good people. We must come to see that human progress never rolls in on wheels of inevitability. It comes through the tireless efforts and persistent work of men willing to be co-workers with God, and without this hard work itself becomes an ally of the forces of social stagnation. We must use time creatively, and forever realize that the time is always ripe to do right.[9]

Because I believe people are genuinely good, I can only assume that somehow a lot of folks got tuned out. It's time to tune back in, time to take control and change how we treat one another. All it takes is a consistently positive mind-set.

5. Stop, listen, and think — before you speak.

The most frequent complaint I hear about adults from kids is that adults never listen. Listening requires full and conscious attention. To listen, you must be willing to put your needs to the side and take the time to hear. The old adage about counting to ten really works.

I thought I had learned this lesson years before it really took hold. My inclination to speak the truth often frightened and distanced people. I was never questioned about the honesty of my words, it was the delivery that was under scrutiny. I had to learn that being right was not enough. In fact, being right was irrelevant. My manner of presentation was more important than the actual content of my message. What saved me from my own tongue was a thoughtful and quiet boss who took the time to ask questions that demonstrated a need to listen better. Thank God this shift preceded parenthood.

Once as I was leaving on a business trip, my daughter Katy looked at me with her big six-year-old eyes and asked if she could keep my gold chain and locket. My first reaction was to say "No," but I took the time to hear her out. She told me that when I'm gone she sometimes feels lonely and misses me. Instead of disregarding her feelings and telling her how much the necklace cost, I handed it over. When I returned at the end of the week, she was wearing the necklace. She said it made her feel close to me. Had I listened to me, I would have failed her. No possession is more precious than she is to me.

Stop and think about the memories you can make with your responses to your children. Every word you speak is important. Good and bad, every interaction is a potential memory.

6. Focus on the relationship, not the outcome.

Nothing is more valuable than a relationship. Too often we value the product of the relationship more than the experiences between people. When the outcome of a relationship becomes the primary focus, opportunities for enhancing the relationship are missed.

One of the most frequently asked questions I hear from parents is "How can I get my kid to...?" Whether they're referring to chores, curfew, or homework, the parents who ask this question are focusing on the outcome. Likewise, kids report that the only time they have a dialogue with their parents is when something is wrong, needs to be done, or has not yet been completed.

When parents concentrate on how they can get their kid to do something, they are not focusing on the relationship which, in the long run, is much more important that any outcome. Developing and maintaining a relationship takes more time and is more critical to children than demanding specific outcomes. The relationship itself enhances the quality of your life with children and theirs with you. In the long run, the cleanliness of the room doesn't really matter.

7. Breathe.

When you are breathing, harsh words do not come easily. Paying attention to your breathing slows down your kneejerk reactions and gives you time to think. Staying conscious of your breathing creates the opportunity to carefully choose what needs to be said, how you want to say it, and what you might want to request. This simple trick will serve you well. Stop. Breathe. Think. Respond.

8. Experience the moment but focus on the future.

To ensure that the positive attitude is more than words or platitudes, link it to a future vision. (See DOism 3, Focus on the Future, for more about how this works.) Your responses to children shouldn't rehash the past. Each comment or consequence should be related to *what will be* rather than *what has been*. That's how you stay focused on the moment and the future at the same time. Here's an example:

Acknowledge the current reality
I am angry.

Think about the facts or circumstances
She drove drunk.

Determine the message you want to convey
She set up a potentially dangerous situation for herself and others. She broke a nonnegotiable rule for access to the car. She lied and willfully broke a rule.

Stay future focused
You will lose your driving privileges for a minimum of three weeks. Your choice has lead me to believe that you need help in making choices. You will regain the privilege to drive after you create evidence that you can make

choices that do not endanger your life as well as the safety of others.

9. Attempt to forecast how your behavior will be interpreted.

First check your motivation. Is your behavior consistent and congruent with your beliefs? Then try to anticipate the various ways kids may interpret your behavior. Behave and speak in ways that make clear why you are doing what you are doing. If you can see that your actions might be misinterpreted, take special care to define your actions with words. Then ask for feedback. "What did you hear me say? Does this fit with your expectations? Tell me how you feel about what I have said."

I HAVE HEARD MANY children say they believe that the future doesn't matter, that there will be no life after adolescence, and that they can't ever do enough to please their parents or teachers. Each of these scenarios is evidence of a negative mind-set, one that will create immobility and angst. The circumstances of their lives have been interpreted negatively. Our job is to help them turn around their interpretations. "The game of life is not so much in holding a good hand as playing a poor hand well."[10]

Notes

1. Albert Einstein, paraphrased by Margaret J. Wheatley in *Leadership and the New Science: Learning About Organization from an Orderly Universe* (San Francisco: Berrett-Koehler Publishers, 1992), p. 5. The original Einstein quote is in *Quotes and Quips*

(Provo, UT: Covey Leadership Center, Inc., 1993): "The significant problems we face cannot be solved at the same level of thinking we were at when we created them."

2. Shad Helmstetter, *What to Say When You Talk to Your Self* (New York: Simon & Schuster, 1986), p. 21.

3. Ed Oakley and Doug Krug, *Enlightened Leadership: Getting to the Heart of Change* (Denver: Stone Tree Publishing, 1991).

4. Ibid., p. 40. Reprinted with permission.

5. Ibid., p. 64–65. Reprinted with permission.

6. George Bernard Shaw, *Mrs. Warren's Profession* (Act II), quoted in *Familiar Quotations,* John Bartlett and Emily Morrison Beck, eds. (Boston: Little, Brown and Company, 1980), p. 680.

7. David McNally, *Even Eagles Need a Push: Learning to Soar in a Changing World* (New York: Delacorte Press, 1990), p. 146.

8. Warren Bennis and Joan Goldsmith, *Learning to Lead: A Workbook on Becoming a Leader* (Reading, MA: Addison-Wesley, 1994), p. 139.

9. Martin Luther King, Jr., quoted in Warren Bennis and Joan Goldsmith, *Learning to Lead: A Workbook on Becoming a Leader* (Reading, MA: Addison-Wesley, 1994), p. 141.

10. H. T. Leslie, quoted in *Peter's Quotations: Ideas for Our Time,* Laurence J. Peter, ed. (New York: Bantam, 1979), p. 308.

Embrace Change

Everything changes but change itself.
— John F. Kennedy[1]

Many adults consider the achievement of stability as their ultimate life goal. Unfortunately, maintaining stability is practically impossible in these rapidly changing times, and pursuing a permanent state can actually be harmful. When goals are unreachable, stress and frustration can quickly replace hope and drive.

Change is occurring so quickly that much of what we buy today is out of date by the time we get it home. This year's technology has made obsolete the computer you purchased just last year. Many of the futurists and organizational development experts use technology as a yardstick for change because as technology changes humans must adapt. With our phenomenal technological progression, this means flexibility is a prime quality for the future.

In family therapy, a story is often told about the woman who cooks the Sunday roast in two pans. Her husband seeks to understand why his new wife insists on cutting the roast in two before cooking it. He talks to her mom, who says, "That's just the way we do it. My mother did it that way." Then he talks to the grandmother, and she laughs and reminisces about how she never had a roasting pan big enough for the roast that fed her family of six children. Her solution was to cut the roast in two and cook it in two pans, a solution that was never questioned and lasted three generations.

Holding on to the way things have been is often a product of habit and routine rather than conscious choice or real need. Since we choose how we view current experiences, thereby creating our own reality, we must realize our options. We can create our reality from our past, or we can choose to open ourselves to new ways of thinking and acting.

Are you a keeper of the past or are you a willing adventurer looking toward the future? Two common signs of those who refuse to embrace change are *denial* (refusing to see) and *resistance* (fighting the forces that demand some change occur). Denial and resistance are powerful forces, often leading to personal pain for those who resist change as well as their loved ones. Rather than struggling with these demons, my advice is to view change as a positive force, an opportunity to make things better.

I have come to understand that I must strive to create systems that are flexible and responsive to circumstances while developing stable relationships. In the past I thought the systems had to be stable and the relationships flexible. I'm not the only one. My evidence? Divorce. Abductions. Racism. Anger and hate crimes. In the pursuit of the elusive stability, we have lost sight of the fact that the quality of our lives is best reflected by the relationships we keep. Change should affect our systems and support our relationships.

Michael Fullan, an advocate for educational reform and author of *Change Forces: Probing the Depths of Educational Reform*, offers some information essential to a clear understanding of what it means to live a life that embraces the future. I have adapted Fullan's work to make it applicable to adult-child relationships.[2]

Five Realities of Embracing Change

I have named these the "five realities of embracing change" because each seems to answer the rationales for why people who choose to stay the same always have logical excuses. Each of the five realities combines to create forces that will make change more palatable and possible, and each is a truism that offers a DOism challenge.

1. You cannot mandate what matters to others.

People must *feel* right to *do* right. "Good" behavior cannot be legislated. However, you *can* create opportunities where being good will be valued and noted. The best way to have children internalize what you value is to model those values. If you want them to value school, for example, then you need to reinforce learning and educational opportunities.

2. Uncertainty can create excitement.

Many adults long for stability, but they often confuse *stability* with *comfort*. Every stage of a relationship with a child is uncertain. Uncertainty can be part of *comfort* — if it is embraced instead of avoided. Those who embrace uncertainty can start to enjoy the moment. With the acceptance that every new experience can be met as a new possibility, excitement will follow.

3. "Mistakes," "problems," and "failure" are feedback.

Children need to see that "mistakes" are nothing more than a missed guess, a miscalculation-calculation. What we call "mistakes," "problems," and "failures" are actually the opportunities that can breed strength rather than hopelessness.

(For more information about the value of "mistakes," see DOism 4.)

4. Personal mind-sets often thwart change.

Being set in your ways, being unwilling to hear new opinions, and being upset when things are out of your control all indicate mind-set paralysis. Rigidity in any form can (and often does) engender pathology.

It is important to note the difference between rigidity and nonnegotiables. *Rigidity* is an unwillingness to listen or negotiate. *Nonnegotiables* are standards that an individual chooses as specific boundaries for behavior.

An architect friend nearly lost his job because of his unwillingness to use a computer for certain aspects of his job. That's rigid. I choose not to serve alcohol at social events in my home. That's a nonnegotiable. In parenting and in teaching, the difference between these two elements is noteworthy. Kids will respect nonnegotiables, but they will rebel against rigidity. The quality of your relationship and your attitude is often what will color the difference.

5. An internal shift must take place before an external change in behavior can occur.

Change is a highly personalized experience. Without an internal shift, an external behavioral change is often short-lived. Very few New Year's resolutions are held all year. Change is a process, not an event — a slow process that allows you to gradually get used to the shift in thinking, believing, and behaving. Like profound learning, change is permanent when it is emotionally charged. This requires an internal inventory.

EACH OF THESE FIVE REALITIES can be internalized to facilitate positive change processes. Here are some examples:

> Before she can hand over the controls of her daughter's wardrobe, a mother must recognize her teenage daughter's need to be in charge of some aspects of her life. She has to shift from *"I* must approve of your clothes" to *"You* are in charge of choosing appropriate clothes for different kinds of activities."

> When a father relinquishes his desire to choose his six-year-old son's friends, he creates an opportunity for the boy to discover what he wants in a friend. Left to his own devices and with gentle guidance, the boy learns about his own preferences and how to interpret character from outward behavior.

Both of these parents changed their beliefs of what parenting *should* be. Parents often operate on a model linked to their past: "My parents behaved like this with me and therefore these rules are good enough for you." This mode of thinking can be harmful. The rapid pace of change is widening the generation gap. This generation of children has few experiences in common with their parents. Connections are built on similarities. When parents are unable to develop meaningful connections, the entire relationship is thwarted.

The way out of this dilemma must be initiated by the parents, who have to let go of their past and redirect their attention to how they want to be in the future. When parents and teachers shift to supporting the future, they profoundly influence the quality of their relationships with children. The only thing adults need to do is give up their shoulds based on the past and focus on what can be! Take note:

A teacher presents a prepared lesson to a group of second graders. She ignores the fact that the kids have had no recess three days in a row because of rain. They are also looking forward to a classroom party scheduled for that afternoon. Even though the kids are squirrely, the teacher sticks to the lesson plan. The afternoon is tense for teacher and students alike. If she had met the kids where they were rather than trying to force them to meet her, she would have made great strides in creating a meaningful exchange with her students.

This scenario underscores the need to stay in the moment and be flexible. When we become comfortable with change, when we embrace it instead of running from it, new positive life experiences will occur. Life becomes a responsive dance that fosters acceptance rather than resistance, thereby creating viable new ways of being. You are in control, even within the context of changing your mind. In fact, your ability to change your mind is the greatest evidence of your personal power!

In *Leadership and the New Science*, Margaret J. Wheatley describes how you can make the most out of your experiences with change.[3] Here is a summary of the things she urges us to remember:

- Most people want to do and be good.
- Diversity provides opportunities.
- Solutions must be responsive to the moment. As context changes, so will the solutions.
- Change is best when it creates something specific for a given situation; models created elsewhere won't always work.

• Reality changes because of what we are doing now. When we focus on what we are doing, we are more likely to create a positive reality.

• Whatever we focus on will expand.

These six conditions provide a dimension to the change process. Change can make something better, provide opportunities, allow for creativity, and acknowledge the new reality created from the change.

To truly embrace change, we must move through five steps.

Unconsciousness
"Nothing needs to change."

Preconsciousness
"Something might need to change."

Awareness
"I know what needs to be done to create change."

Choice
"I know what I'll DO."

Action
"I will DO it."

The most challenging hurdles are from awareness to choice and from choice to action. The difficulties we experience in translating our choices into action have befuddled social scientists for years. How can people know what needs to be done yet be unwilling to make the necessary changes that are the prerequisites for change?

If we could answer that one question, we would have remedies for AIDS, teen pregnancy, addiction, and divorce. Social problems are not growing so much because of a lack of knowledge, but because of a lack of awareness and an inability to act. Kids *know* they should use condoms, yet they *choose* not to. As a result, the rate of teen pregnancy is astronomical while the rate of teen HIV infection is growing at an alarming rate.

Change is tough. For most, staying the same is easier than taking the necessary steps to make the change a reality. Those who refuse to embrace change set off chains of events that often perpetuate pain and engender adversity. A willingness to become change-friendly can improve the quality of life.

After I read Margaret Wheatley's *Leadership and the New Science*, I felt as though we can all truly affect the quality of our lives simply by acknowledging that we are all an interconnected whole. Understanding that the entire universe is dynamically energized by interactions that can change reality has freed me to be a willing change agent, someone who has the ability to create something that never existed before. Change literally motivates evolution, and my ability to keep up is the impetus for how I choose to live. Trying to stay the same doesn't work. Invisible forces compel movement. I would rather be in charge of change than be its puppet.

The key to staying in charge of change is an awareness of and a cognitive appreciation for the beliefs that motivate behavior. The best way to stay mentally healthy is to live as you believe — walk your talk. Change is responsive to core beliefs (your talk) framed by current experiences and behavior (your walk). An important aspect of quality relationships with children is the ability to be with them in their current experience. Your best chance to influence children is through a caring and nurturing relationship, embracing each new experience as an opportunity to learn.

The change phenomenon is not elusive. Take it out of the realm of something you have to DO and move it into choice, challenge, and opportunity. Two common areas of behavior thwart change: (1) fear, and (2) rigid or unexamined beliefs.

Both tend to consume motivation. Many of us are paralyzed: dissatisfied with the status quo but unwilling to DO what is necessary to embrace change.

The process of change needs to be demystified. Change can become a friend to nurture rather than a monster to fear. The nemesis of change is relapse — returning to old and familiar patterns. When relapse occurs, people tend to blame change for their difficulties. Change does interrupt what have become normal processes. Initially, living with change is abnormal — it feels as if the normal thing to DO would be to return to the old, familiar ways.

How does this relate to your relationships with children? Today's children have nothing to do with your past. Your life experiences and their life experiences share few common points. To truly embrace a child, you must be willing to also embrace change. An adult who serves a child best is willing to meet in the child's reality. Change is vital to raising and educating children. Being successful requires the coupling of a willingness to embrace change with an ability to sort to the positive. This will create a special relationship upon which children can be guided and mentored.

The next DOism, Focus on the Future, contributes the missing piece in the triangulation of ingredients needed to contribute positively to a child's life: sort to the positive, embrace change, and look to the future. The future is the reality all children must be prepared to embrace. In the future, we want them to thrive.

Notes

1. John F. Kennedy, from a speech given May 19, 1963, Vanderbilt University, quoted in *Contemporary Quotations*, James B. Simpson, ed. (New York: Crowell, 1964), p. 26.

2. Michael Fullan, *Change Forces: Probing the Depths of Educational Reform* (London: Falmer Press, 1993). The first and third of my "Five Realities of Embracing Change" are the first and third of Fullan's "Eight Basic Lessons of the New Paradigm of Change," pp. 21–22, May 1994 special edition of *Change Forces* for the California Alliance for Elementary Education.

3. Margaret Wheatley, *Leadership and the New Science: Learning About Organization from an Orderly Universe* (San Francisco: Berrett-Koehler, 1992).

Focus on the Future

Life can only be understood backwards;
but it must be lived forwards.
— Søren Kierkegaard[1]

Even though the future is difficult to predict, we must prepare for it. Ralph Stacey, a British management consultant and writer, has provided innumerable directions for managing the future. In *Managing the Unknowable,* Stacey maintains that we must accept the following future realities.[2]

1. No one can have control of the future.

2. The direction we take must emerge as a consequence of our relationships coupled with the current circumstance.

3. The process of change must allow the direction to emerge and requires that we embark without the safety of a map.

4. The future will be a response to what we are doing now.

5. The future can be impacted by creativity.

6. Models that attempt to understand and forecast the future have moved from order, stability, and consistency to an acceptance of chance, change, and chaos. This movement requires close attention to the patterns and fluctuations that occur naturally. Goals and forecasts are important, but the experience garnered as the goal is pursued is even more valuable.

To prepare for the unknowable, then, all we can do is develop the skills and traits we strongly suspect will be required: flexibility, sociability, and skills related to communication, critical thinking, and interpersonal relationships. We cannot depend upon lessons from the past. Too much emphasis on the past often creates a cycle of repetition and embellishment. While our history has significant value, it is not the only available lens for viewing the future. Another view, proposed by the quantum physicists George Land and Beth Jarman, allows tomorrow to be pulled by the future.[3] We have to be responsive and realistic, and we need to take risks.

Children who survive tough circumstances balance the stress of their current experience by focusing on the future. This coping strategy seems to mitigate the pressing difficulties of the present. It also provides a sense of hope, a mechanism for choice, and a willingness to delay gratification. A child choosing for the future makes a very different decision than a child who is unable to foresee a future reality. Many of the children I have worked with were unable to see beyond the torment of the present reality. Their gang decisions, drug choices, promiscuity, and school failure were easily explained by their lack of future sight.

The kids who survive adversity have a very different perspective. They say, "My mom is sick and I have to take care of her, but I am planning to go to college so I will be able to earn my own living." Resilient children see the future in terms of opportunities, strive to make the situation better, and see improvement as a possibility. They operate from an internal dialogue that prevents them from being stuck in the now while helping them see the possibilities the future holds for them.

Helping a child focus on what *can be* is hard. Developmentally, the very nature of children belies attending to anything beyond the immediate circumstance. Children actually must be *taught* to concentrate on what *might* occur. Numerous stories provide children with the opportunity to see the value of sustaining a future focus. My favorite, *Uncle Jed's Barbershop,* is the story of a man who through periods of gross and chronic adversity still believes in his dream.[4] At age 79 Uncle Jed reaches his goal — and dies shortly thereafter. Read this book to your kids!

One aspect of that learning can be addressed through effective questioning. Try these questions to help a child start looking to the future.

1. What do you think you will need to know when you are my age?

2. What pleases you most about your life now?

3. What are your goals? What will you need to reach your goals? What might get in your way? What can you do now to remove these obstacles?

4. What is your evidence that you are growing up? By what criteria do you judge yourself? Who is grown up? What do you respect about them? How does your respect for them affect you?

5. What are your abilities? Where did they come from? Who is in control of the skills you develop?

Notice that the questions *don't* ask, "What do you think will happen?" Instead, each question is designed to start a dialogue about what the child perceives, thinks, and understands. You can then ask questions linked to a specific forecast. Engage in the repartee, a communication dance that allows the child to lead as well as follow.

Too often the adult-child relationship is fraught with top-down communication. When it comes to the future children must feel as though what will happen is in their control.

Fostering dialogue is one of the best ways to initiate a pull to the future. The more real and hopeful the future becomes, the more positive energy it will be given.

Children think about what will be all the time. As adults, we need to learn how to tap into their internal dialogue and support them. Children create private places where their ideas about the future reside. Very often they are worried about appearing stupid and choose silence as a defense. Once you start young people talking, you'll be amazed at what they have figured out on their own. (My daughter once told me she knew God wasn't real because no one seemed to have his phone number. Made sense to her.)

What and *how* questions are the most likely to solicit information. *Why* questions almost always conjure up defenses. Silence helps. Kids don't process information as quickly as adults. Slow down for them. Besides, many kids are not used to being solicited to talk. If you slow the pace, you give them one of your most precious commodities — time.

Three basic questions can shape your discussions of the future with a child:

- How does the dynamic nature of development underscore what is happening to me?
- Are my healthy and positive expectations defined by cause and effect?
- Do I create ways to prepare for the future by what I do today?

Let's look at each dimension.

The Dynamic Nature of Development

Children do not seem to understand fully that they are constantly growing and changing. That's why they like to hear stories of when they were little and why they like to check their height so often. Children need adults to gain a realistic perspective about their personal growth. They need to understand their personal development and we need to understand their perceptions. My daughter has helped me understand this paradox. While I look at her as my little girl, she views herself as quite grown-up.

On her seventh birthday, I found her cleaning out her closet. I asked her what she was doing and she announced she had to get rid of most of her clothes because they were not "old enough" for her new position in life. I had no idea she viewed seven as a life-changing age, while she had no idea I wanted her to stay my baby as long as possible. I let her box up the clothes, but when she realized that taking them out of her closet didn't mean she would get new ones she put them back.

Adults are constantly confronted with the changes children experience. They see how fast a child grows because they have to buy the clothes. They monitor their children's progress and see the evidence of the changes almost daily. For the adult, the growth of children often precipitates a sense of loss, while the child feels the excitement of change. A common error in the relationship between children and adults is the expectation that both share the same reality. If a parent knows her daughter is changing, the daughter *should* have the same knowledge.

Not true. Children often are unable to perceive themselves outside their current experience. Helping children understand that they are in a dynamic and powerful process of ongoing change serves as the basis for staying future-focused.

To help children in this process, adults can do several things:

• Display photographs and play videotapes that show
  obvious growth in the child.

- Write observations in a journal, and periodically read old entries to the child.

- Create ways to look back in time. Note physical changes. Attend to interest shifts. Watch and comment on the external changes of others. Look at the young-old continuum in literature, TV, and in the neighborhood.

- Have dialogues that encourage self-reflection. Ask questions that allow for personal inventory. How did you feel? What did you think they felt?

- Provide opportunities for cross-age experiences. These experiences can replicate the phenomenon of natural kinship and provide kids with age perspectives.

A child who is future-focused will learn from experiences, discern cause-and-effect relationships, pause to think before making a commitment, and ask cautious questions. Adults can make a difference by modeling reflective dialogue. Talk about mistakes. Talk about how time plays an important role in the process of growth. More than anything, convey that survival is the norm.

Now, on to expectations.

Healthy and Positive Expectations

It is difficult for a child to take on healthy and positive expectations if the idea of developmental growth has not been internalized. Understanding that there is a future must precede preparing for it. This is where DOism 1 (Sort to the Positive) plays an important role. Many young people have internalized a negative view of their future. This view tends to limit their ability to see themselves in another context, time, or situation.

Start at the beginning. "What is the evidence that you'll be okay when you are older?" If that is too advanced, start more simply. "How does what you are learning now prepare you for later life?" In fact, any question that forces a dialogue about what is unknown will serve the child. Something needs to trigger an exchange of what can be versus what is.

I sometimes use time capsules to help teach about the future. I ask the child to play a guessing game with me. We make up prophecies about ourselves, design a holding vessel (the time capsule), place the time capsule in a secure place, decide when we will open it, and then plan our next time together. Use the time capsule at significant transitions and life markers: graduation from junior high or high school, passing a driver's test, college entrance. This process focuses a child on the future, encourages delayed gratification, and helps give the future credence.

Delaying gratification is a significant skill and an important life lesson. Contingency contracting is another way to help a child delay immediate gratification. A contingency contract is a contract where if she does *X,* then you'll do *Y.* Describe the task, the expectations, and establish clear consequences (children will think up better ones than you can, if you ask them). The key to contracting with children is that they need to fill in all the blanks. You make reasonable agreements. They must take ownership of the process and the outcome.

A second dimension of healthy expectations is having positive aspirations. The desire to do or be something drives many toward the future. Positive aspirations foster healthy expectancies and help align how we behave with what we are striving for in the future.

Kids develop healthy expectations when they have healthy role models. Ask yourself, "What view of the future do I portray?" Check the emotional range that you regularly share with the children in your world. Happy? Sad? Angry? Frustrated? Distraught? Fretful? Joyful?

Kids are our mirrors. Listen to their words. Observe their behavior. They tell you everything you need to know if you are tuned in. Tired, frustrated, overworked adults have a hard time tuning in. The adults in a child's life and the nature of the child's relationship with these adults will foster the kind of expectations that the child will internalize and create.

By the way, healthy expectations are not necessarily planned by the adults in a child's life. Children need to plan their own lives with support and guidance from the adults around them. Children will survive their decisions, learn to ask for help if needed, and keep on the track that makes them happy.

Many would say this approach seems overly simplistic, but getting to the point where this is possible is not simple. The relationship is the key to success in working, living, and being with children. Children with low self-esteem do not think of themselves as having low self-esteem. More than likely all they know is that their life seems less than somebody else's. Low self-esteem is a label used by an outsider who views the whole of someone's life. No children, in my career, ever presented esteem as their problem. Mothers who are too critical, absent fathers, loneliness, ugliness, hopelessness — these are the problems of kids who feel *less than.*

Nobody makes anybody DO anything. Granted, some people — children and adults — are unable to see their choices, but somewhere along the line, choices mold behavior, and that behavior always has some personal benefit.

All kids living under difficult circumstances do not find inappropriate outlets for their energy and drive. Many kids have had caring and nurturing adults pull them into activities that put these kids in the driver's seat. This is not a simple approach; it demands that adults risk their own vulnerability, go where others have not dared to go, and allow themselves to be an integral part of a kid's life. The kids who survive adversity speak often of the adults who cared, persevered, and helped them be happy.

Make sure that your relationships with children give them permission to be happy, playful, and aware of others. Children need to create their happiness in their own way. We merely help frame healthy and positive choices.

Now, on to creativity.

Creative Ways to Prepare for the Future

The best way to plan for the future, according to Stephen Covey, is to create it.[5] Peter Drucker, a management expert, agrees.[6] The only obstacle that prevents most of us from creating our future is our "shoulds." I hate shoulds. More trouble is caused by shoulds than almost any other human interaction. Let's look at some should dilemmas.

> Mario *should* learn to play the piano. Mario is the only kid on the block who *has* to practice piano, and he is ridiculed for this. He hates practicing piano and he hates being ridiculed. He doesn't want to hurt his mom. He feels guilty. He has started to create fights just before he is supposed to practice so that he is punished instead. The *should* isn't working.

> Susie *should* study. Her siblings all read well and fast. Susie doesn't. She thinks everybody is reading every word and remembering everything. Susie doesn't know they all have tricks to read fast. She thinks she is dumb because she *should* be able to read like everybody else. She worries so much about reading that she never gets to do the things she's really good at, like music and math. Smart people *should* be able to read fast. The *should* isn't helping.

Billy is deaf. Even though research indicates he will do
better if he is in a regular classroom, the parents of some
of Billy's classmates insist he *should* be in a special class.

In each of these scenarios, the people who say "should"
see no reason why their reality shouldn't be imposed on others, yet an imposed loss of rights follows this assumption.
A child needs to be understood, not "shoulded." Making
choices is the one true freedom. When I am allowed to choose,
I am allowed to dictate what my future might be. At the very
least, I am able to discern a direction that is appropriate for
me. I am in control of my fate through a choosing process.

Choice is vital for quality of life. Learn to play the piano.
Read your way. Take your kid out of a class. You have
choices. The limits that you internalize are validated in your
own mind. But what if you don't know you have choices?
Nothing will change until you feel discomfort, which can
shake the foundation of your beliefs. Then change is possible.

Many adults talk about understanding their children's
need to make choices, and then they condemn the choices
made. Helping kids create their future has to be on *their* terms.
It is *their* future. Your children have nothing to do with your
past, so stop imposing it. You will never experience their future as they do, but you can encourage them to be prepared.

Prepare for what you know and expect to discover what
you don't know. Stay open, aware, and alive. Help children
look for patterns. Help them focus on the nuances of their relationships. Ask appropriate questions: How do you interact
with others? How does this interaction affect you? What is
your best guess of what will happen? What is your evidence
of this best guess? Who are your resources? Are they valid
and reliable? Is what you think reasonable? Does it align with
your beliefs and your intuition?

Build personal experiences that will support the future.

Most people involved in business in the twenty-first century will need to speak Spanish. Instead of waiting for a mandate or requirement, learn Spanish now and teach it to your children. Since technology drives human change, stay on top of technology as it relates to your field and make this technology available to your children. Help your children develop a world consciousness, since we are moving toward a worldwide economy. No experience is ever wasted; if your projections are wrong, you are left with good information.

Six Ways to Focus on the Future

Most adults are not aware of the powerful beliefs they pass on to children. From adults children learn everything from the value of money and material things to how others should be treated. We can make a difference in our children and in our society by emphasizing what we want our children to learn. To secure the future of our children, we must embrace and exemplify the following principles:

1. Create opportunities for all people to engage in meaningful work.

Meaningful work can be described as activities that promote learning and a positive sense of self. When children do not have something meaningful to do, it is difficult for them to develop a sense of competency.

2. Foster a consciousness that values all people.

Equitable opportunities and respect for all are the basis of a positive prosocial consciousness. Somehow we need to help our children look at each other as resources and possible colleagues instead of competitors and possible enemies. Nothing is more limiting than a perception that one kind of person is less than or more than another.

3. Place a high value on using information to benefit all people.

Information must be used for the betterment of all people — this is the essence of cooperation. Information should improve the quality of life, foster decisions, and make things clearer. Everyone should have access to information. Too often children are not exposed to certain types of information. What they don't know they make up, and what they make up suits their understanding of what is going on.

4. Support humanitarian efforts.

All living things must be valued. Somehow valuing and protecting the human condition must be elevated to a task evidencing greatness. Heroes could be made of those who achieve humanitarian greatness. It's easy to support children doing well for others, but you must also be involved.

5. Value sacrifice for the betterment of the whole.

Sacrifice is a yesterday value that needs to be reinvented for this generation. Kids need to view their circumstances in terms of personal power. A product of any focused journey, sacrifice is what must be given up to achieve.

6. Demand that rights and responsibilities be linked.

This generation has seen too little connection between rights and responsibilities. Kids tend to view their rights as inalienable without prescribing the innate responsibilities that link the two. The linkage between rights and responsibilities must be articulated inside a process that is comprehensible to children. As they grow, the responsibilities become greater while the rights stay constant. Table 3.1 shows how these rights and responsibilities might read.

Table 3.1 The Rights and Responsibilities of Children

The Rights of Children	The Responsibilities of Children
You have the right to discovery.	All discovery must be considered in terms of its value to humankind.
You have the right to speak your mind.	Speaking out must never intentionally hurt someone else.
You have the right to express your feelings.	Your feelings are yours to vent and experience, but they must never be used to create pain for someone else.
You have the right to safety.	You must choose activities that will protect your safety.
You have the right to caring adults.	Caring, nurturing adults can be found in all walks of life; you are responsible for seeking sources of support.
You have the right to aspire to great heights.	You are limited to what you work for and strive to make real.
You have the right to meaningful opportunities.	Opportunities are best discovered by a conscious spirit that views the world in terms of what can be done.
You have the right to learn from your mistakes.	Every situation is a potential lesson if you are willing to discern it.
You have the right to be heard.	Being heard does not mean that you are always right. Being heard involves a process of reciprocity.
You have the right to express outrage if these rights are not honored.	Speak of your outrage in ways that are not violent and do not impinge upon the rights of others.

WHY ARE THESE PRINCIPLES so important? Our kids need boundaries that are real, our society needs hope for all, and our world needs investment in the future. We must take charge of how we are because we are not in charge of what will be. If these principles were accepted, all of our children would be safe and allowed to prosper. While not one of them is likely to be fully realized, each provides a direction for how we can believe and behave.

Notes

1. Søren Kierkegaard, quoted in *Even Eagles Need a Push: Learning to Soar in a Changing World* by David McNally (New York: Delacorte, 1990), p. 2.

2. Ralph D. Stacey, *Managing the Unknowable: Strategic Boundaries Between Order and Chaos in Organizations* (San Francisco: Jossey-Bass, 1992).

3. George Land and Beth Jarman, *Break-point and Beyond: Mastering the Future — Today* (New York: HarperBusiness, 1992).

4. Margaret King Mitchell, *Uncle Jed's Barbershop* (New York: Simon & Schuster, 1993).

5. Stephen Covey, *The Seven Habits of Highly Effective People* (New York: Simon & Schuster, 1989).

6. Peter F. Drucker, *Managing for the Future: The 1990s and Beyond* (New York: Dutton, 1992).

DOISM 4

Use Mistakes
and Problems
As Information

Failure is, in a sense, the highway to success,
inasmuch as every discovery of what is false
leads us to seek earnestly after what is true.
— John Keats[1]

Too often, mistakes and problems are viewed as evidence of failure. When failure accumulates, it becomes an obstacle to overcome. Our responsibility as the adults in kids' lives is to help make sense out of failure. Mistakes and problems should be seen as feedback rather than failure — feedback that we didn't plan well, that we didn't think something through, or that we needed more information. To label mistakes and problems as failure is to promote failed experiences. Failure is much more difficult to overcome than mistakes.

A great way to increase a child's understanding that mistakes are valuable learning tools is by asking them some essential questions (without judgment):

- What did you learn from this?
- What would you do differently next time?
- What worked? What didn't? Why?
- What didn't you expect?

• If you were giving advice, what would you recommend to others as a way of avoiding what happened to you?

Each of these questions will help a child use the mistake or the problem as fodder for lessons to be learned. Rather than telling children what they did wrong or why they are wrong, asking these questions initiates a dialogue and preserves the relationship.

To use mistakes and problems as anything more than feedback and information is to create a diabolical monster that grows the more you focus on it. Whether you're a mature adult or a floundering child, if you feel anxious about your ability to do something, if you dwell on how tough the task is or how you can't do it very well, your performance will get worse. This allows too many kids to stop trying; they find it easier to be bad than struggle to become capable. Bad buys them allies, alibis, and excuses.

Using mistakes and problems as feedback and information requires certain resolutions or beliefs:

All behavior has both a purpose and a benefit.
People act the way they do for a reason, but the benefit and purpose of behavior often lie hidden under the surface of reality. Most children and many adults are not aware of their motivations. When we come to understand the benefit or purpose of our own behavior, we start the journey toward self-understanding. When we come to understand the benefit or purpose of a child's behavior, we are able to directly meet the child's needs. This, in turn, enhances the relationship. (For more information about this resolution, see my second basic assumption about kids — all kids behave in ways that benefit them — on page 4.)

Stay in control by choosing your responses.
Make sure that how you respond in any relationship reflects your feelings and accurately presents your con-

cerns. Timing seems to provide the best insurance that the message, the intent, and the interaction are congruent. Taking time to respond is imperative.

Take responsibility.
It's easy to give away personal power. It's even easier to give away responsibility. To encourage and support individual responsibility, we must stop assigning rationales for our behavior to others.

Put people first.
Nothing is more important than the relationship.

A common error in parenting relationships results from demanding external performances without internal acceptance or understanding. Many parents insist on a clean room or good grades — external performances. The more they insist on controlling the outcome, the bigger "the problem" becomes. What they focus on expands.

I have seen families in therapy with a presenting problem of "getting the chores done." Somehow, *not* getting the chores done was allowed to interfere with the entire relationship. Often, control is the issue, disguised as a behavior or attitude problem. The problem-solving process fails because it is impossible to correct a misidentified problem. No matter what is done, the problem continues, unresolved.

Often parents fail to understand that the problems they have with their children are based on something larger than chores or grades. They try to fix what is causing the difficulty, but since they haven't changed their overriding expectations the problem continues — and maybe even escalates.

To change the outcome, the *adult* needs to change, and the child must be allowed to participate in the change process. Discovery is the variable necessary for sustained effort. The child must *discover* the value of getting "it" done the right way.

This reframing is called a paradigm shift — a new way of thinking, behaving, and doing. All that you know, think, and have experienced in a specific area creates your model (paradigm) about how to behave and what to expect. When the paradigm becomes obsolete, a shift to a new model or a new set of expectations can help solve the problem. Stephen Covey writes about paradigm shifts in *The Seven Habits of Highly Effective People.*

Paradigms are powerful because they create the lens through which we see the world. The power of a paradigm shift is the essential power of quantum change, whether that shift is an instantaneous or a slow and deliberate process.[2]

For example, most parents establish certain rules and expectations for children based on the way their parents raised them. When children fail to behave according to this established paradigm, they are judged in terms of obsolete norms.

When the paradigm shifts, everything starts over. Regardless of your investment in the old paradigm, you are going back to zero. You must begin at the beginning! This phenomenon is the hardest to accept. Most folks want to start changing where they are most comfortable. That is, a father in turmoil with his daughter often does not want to hear how he has contributed to the present difficulty. More often, he wants to start where he is most comfortable — discussing the problems the daughter has caused.

I remember well one family I worked with when I was a new therapist under supervision. After eight hour-long sessions over a period of eight weeks, I thought that I had been particularly successful. As we began our ninth session, I welcomed the family with a "How nice it is to see everyone." In response, the youngest child piped up, "We're *not* all here." I looked around and counted. It seemed to me everyone was present. My puzzled look prompted the child to clarify his statement. "My dad kicked my brother out of the house two years ago because he had a boyfriend."

Dismay only mildly describes my reaction. I was so sure that I knew what was going on in the family, that we were working well together, and that they had made remarkable progress. The family had steered our conversations toward topics they felt comfortable discussing without relating the circumstances that contributed to their problems. No matter how effective I thought I was as a therapist, the therapy had been thwarted. We had to redo dialogues to discover new insights that could create a shift in behavior. The first step was changing how the family was thinking about therapy. Next, we had to view the family's problems in light of the truth. Only then could we move into developing realistic strategies for the future.

Understanding the dynamics of the paradigm shift helps to reduce sabotage. This understanding creates a focus in terms of solutioning — what is it going to take to get where you want to be? People who are willing to shift their paradigms enjoy personal gain and are usually motivated more by the heart than the head.

Three Ways to Turn Mistakes into Information

No problem is too big to be solved. Judgments and criticism are not a part of this process. When it comes to relationships with children, discussion and opportunities are necessary ingredients for on-going support. These three steps show how you can open a discussion and offer help. You can't stop action, but you can ask the child to review cause and effect, and to take a new action.

1. Stop. Breathe.

Breathing helps to relax you. Relaxed, you are most likely to make good decisions. Focusing on your breathing slows you down and you are less likely to be overwhelmed. Breathing buys time so that you can respond genuinely.

2. Ask, "Are you okay?"

When answered in the affirmative, go to #3 below. When answered in the negative, say: "Help me understand...." "I'm worried that...." "Know that I want to help."

3. Ask, "What can I do to help?"

Notice that the response process doesn't ask "Why?" and doesn't say "I told you." The focus is not on what happened. Rather, asking "What can I do to help?" shifts attention from the problem/mistake to a feelings-solutions concern that will lead to dialogue and a strengthening of the relationship.

Aᴅᴜʟᴛs ɴᴇᴇᴅ ᴛᴏ ᴇɴsᴜʀᴇ that mistakes are not viewed as evidence of failure but as evidence of an error in forecasting, problem solving, or perspective. When children learn that mistakes give them information about how to perform better, they learn a skill that will serve them forever.

Notes

1. John Keats, quoted in *Even Eagles Need a Push: Learning to Soar in a Changing World* by David McNally (New York: Delacorte, 1990), p. 7.

2. Stephen R. Covey, *The Seven Habits of Highly Effective People* (New York: Simon & Schuster's Fireside edition, 1989), p. 32.

Set Up the Child to Win

*High courage and consideration are both essential
to the win-win. It is the balance that is the real mark
of maturity. If I have it, I can listen,
I can empathically understand,
but I can also courageously confront.*
— Stephen Covey[1]

Stephen Covey is a master at explaining why win-win situations are so critical in human interaction. In *The Seven Habits of Highly Effective People,* he stresses that clarifying expectations with integrity and trust is required to make a win-win possible. "Win-win is a belief in a third alternative," Covey writes. "It's not your way or my way; it's a *better* way...."[2] The key principle in the establishment of a win-win situation is the willingness to relinquish doing things "your way." Self-righteousness has no place in this DOism.

We need to set up win-win situations in all our relationships. Anything less is a missed opportunity. Can kids always win? Yes. Circumstances can be brought to bear that allow the child an opportunity to win. I am not talking about letting a child win. Children are far too sophisticated to tolerate an adult who cheats. Win-wins are not products of dishonesty. Rather, a win-win manifests solutions that are acceptable to everybody.

Win-win goes beyond a specified outcome into our perceptions and mind-sets. Win-win relationships are grounded in trust and rely on the ability to cooperate, collaborate, and affiliate. Integrity is birthed by win-win interactions that are fostered by the prosocial skills of cooperation, collaboration, and affiliation.

The major objection I hear when I talk about this phenomenon is that a win-win life will not replicate the realities of the real world. Over and over I hear these comments:

"People cheat and lie."

"They'll get ya."

"Kids need to be prepared for the disappointments of life."

I disagree. I believe that children with a history of winning will be well-prepared to manage whatever they are dealt. I also believe that life is a reflection of how we choose to respond to the situations we confront. A win-win provides the fodder for dealing effectively with life. I am convinced that losing doesn't teach positive and supportive lessons. Most often kids discern that losing translates to loser, winning to winner. Which would you choose?

This basic concept is hard for some people to grasp because we have been brought up in a competitive world where someone usually wins at someone else's expense. Suppose that instead of discovering who does best, we find out what each individual does well? No comparisons are made. We equalize the playing field, so to speak. We do not weigh one player against another. This is the beginning of changing the mind-set from loser-avoidance to winning-acceptance. Others agree.

> *I believe that if one man gains spiritually, the whole world gains with him, and if one man falls, the whole world falls to that extent. I do not help my opponents without at the same time helping myself and my co-workers.*
> — Mahatma Gandhi[3]

Trying to do well and trying to beat others are two different things. Excellence and victory are conceptually distinct ... and are experienced differently.
— Alfie Kohn[4]

Competition sparks our economy and fuels our motivation. Competition defines losers. Competition provides an inherent conflict between all players in all games. Competition is a big part of sports, grades, incentives, stickers, college selections, and child's play. It's everywhere and drives most of the energy that makes up our world.

Somehow we must let go of the competition that has become an American trademark. Competition resembles an addiction. You don't realize that it has taken over your life. You sometimes regret your behavior because of the addiction, and you can't remember a time when it didn't exist. It's fun for a while, but the stakes get higher and higher. Somebody always loses.

We can make cooperation an integral part of how we work with kids. The very nature of cooperation brings people together, equally. Equal opportunities for all are only possible through cooperative ventures. Cooperation is a part of our history and the American tradition.

The shift from competition to cooperation requires more than putting people in groups and asking them to DO something. Cooperation is a manifestation of trust and a desire to get something done. Becoming involved only in those situations where everyone has bought in at the same level prevents sabotage. What do you *do* if the playing field isn't equal? Don't play — or revise the circumstances in such a way that everyone can win.

By now you are probably wondering if this is a viable and reality-based DOism. Do all kids need to win all the time? Is there no value to failure? Let's look at an example.

Annie's teenage daughter signed up for an advanced class at 7 A.M., but (like many teens) she has a hard time getting up in the morning. Annie said to her husband, "If she oversleeps, let her take the consequences. Her grade will go down or she will be marked tardy and have to make up the time after school. I don't want to have to get her up every day. It doesn't teach her to take responsibility."

Annie's father disagreed. "I'll get her up and take her to school," he told his wife.

"This is not our responsibility," Annie insisted.

"For god's sake," Dad countered with anger.

Mom and Dad kept up the argument for half a semester.

Annie asked me how to stop her husband from treating her daughter like a child. "Who signed up for the course?" I asked.

Mom explained that the daughter signed up, but with some reluctance. The girl signed up for the advanced course because her mom thought it would be a good idea.

"So, *you* wanted her to have this class?" I asked.

"Yes," said Annie.

"Then I think your husband has the right idea."

"What?" she said.

"Your husband is on track," I explained. "He is trying to figure out what is needed for your daughter to succeed in this 7 A.M. class. Your daughter has not lived up to your expectations and you resent your husband's intervention. But look, it's working. What was your daughter's grade at the end of the quarter?"

"B."

"If you applaud your husband and daughter for their willingness to work together, then a win-win situation is possible."

A long silence hung over the room. Finally Annie said, "I still think she should get up herself...."

I laughed and said, "Stop *shoulding* on your kid."
She groaned and then smiled. "You're right," she said.

ADULTS AND CHILDREN NEED to come together and build an alliance in order to create win-win situations. Success is contingent upon all players doing their best with integrity and trust. This makes the partnership work. This makes partnerships possible.

This win-win approach eliminates the loser classification. When you have done your best, you never lose. Your perception makes the difference. I teach win-win to children by playing a modified version of tic-tac-toe. According to my rules, you can choose to be an *X* or an *O* at each turn. All the other rules apply. The goal of the game is to do your best; doing your best translates into not losing or winning.

A commitment to win-win requires that you be a source of help and a source of modeling. Left to their own devices, children will engage in win-lose interactions in which they feel good because someone else feels bad. There are some ways to ensure that a win-win occurs.

Setting up kids to win works when the circumstances are under your control. For example, you make decisions that affect the children in your life. You can choose what the child's experience will be by how you organize events and opportunities. One child was quoted by L. Tobin in *What to Do with a Child Like This?* He mused, "Can't you make it a game to include me? You are the only person strong enough to make them see who I am."[5] This child recognizes that adults can manipulate the circumstances to make winning possible.

What do we do when circumstances are out of our control? Winning occurs when we lessen the effect of adversity. Resilient children offer great hope that all children can be set up to win regardless of their personal experiences. The difficulty of their lives is mitigated with future-focused expectations, social competency, the ability to think clearly, and a sense of personal efficacy. This skills repertoire, coupled with high expectations and nurturing adult relationships, can set up winning conditions in spite of troubled circumstances.

Like so many things, winning is in the eye of the beholder. My expectation is not that all children have the same experiences in life. That would be boring and very unrealistic. Rather, my expectation is that we can prepare all children to handle whatever they are dealt in ways that allow them to view themselves as competent and capable — in other words, that all children be winners.

Six Steps to Setting Up Win-Win Situations

1. Establish ground rules.

Make clear what is negotiable and what is not negotiable. Try not to frame rules in the negative. Rules that I like to use are defined in positive terms and tell people what to DO to be successful. The rules outlined in Table 5.1 can apply in varied settings. Notice that these guidelines do not impose specifics, for these must be negotiated with each child.

Let's look at the example of an adolescent child who wants a late curfew. Before a decision is made about what time is appropriate, the parents and the child need to review past agreements in the context of the house rules. Has the child proven to be responsible? Then the community's curfew law for minors needs to be reviewed. Will this curfew be in violation of any law? They might also discuss what will be evidence of responsible management of the curfew (calling

Table 5.1 Nonnegotiable Guidelines

In the Classroom
1. Be prompt.
2. Be prepared.
3. Participate positively.
4. Actively share your ideas.
5. Actively listen to others.
6. Be creative.
7. Be patient.
8. Stay focused.
9. Be hopeful.
10. Look to the future.

At Home
1. Value family.
2. Speak your mind.
3. Be willing to help and offer assistance.
4. Notice the positive.
5. Be honest and apologize when necessary.
6. Strive to do well.
7. Honor others.
8. Take on responsibility.
9. Be safety conscious.
10. Follow the laws.

In Life
1. Accept responsibility.
2. Respect all life forms.
3. Notice beauty.
4. Be kind.
5. Be generous.
6. Value goodness.
7. Acknowledge selfless acts.
8. Look for opportunities to help.
9. Volunteer.
10. Vote.

when plans change, informing of whereabouts, being where the child said she'd be).

The best rules are not imposed, but developed as agreement for a given situation. As circumstances change, review the rules to ensure applicability to the current reality. Don't negotiate the nonnegotiables without making reference to a choice to change and for what reason.

If rules are broken, check out two things:

- Was there an attempt to self-correct?
- Is there any evidence that the rule was broken without cognition?

For example, a child breaks curfew because he rushed a friend to the hospital when they got a call that her dad just had a heart attack. It makes sense that being caught in the moment might preclude remembering to call.

If the rule is maliciously or defiantly broken, immediately honor all prenegotiated consequences. How can you tell the difference? Honor your intuition; it is usually your best barometer. Rules are working when a child self-corrects. The more the child honors your relationship, the more likely the child will tell you the truth about what happened. Rules broken maliciously are evidence of greater problems with the relationship.

2. Focus on how you want the children to be rather than on how they behave.

Children must be validated for doing well and encouraged to BE good. By emphasizing BEING GOOD (as a state of consciousness), DOING GOOD logically follows. I have found it easier to focus on the state of being rather than specific behavior. This gives children choice and control. They are in charge of how they behave as long as it is consistent with the standards that define BEING GOOD.

3. Be cooperative, helpful, and kind.

These three conditions make up my standard for BEING GOOD. Each provides a different dimension of goodness. Cooperation brings people together as they share and strive for common goals. Emphasizing helpfulness challenges everyone to serve others. Kindness reflects a basic expectation for all interpersonal contacts. Focusing on these three elements of BEING GOOD underscores how to DO GOOD.

4. Notice the incremental successes.

All skill development is experienced in stages. Each stage needs to be validated and acknowledged as important. Celebrate the steps toward a goal. By doing so, you are more likely to sustain motivation and keep children focused on the future.

5. Make being and working together fun.

All learning, all work, all pursuits can be fun. Fun doesn't mean that you don't take the task seriously. You can invent the means by which you DO the jobs that are required. For example, when we clean my daughter's room, we do it to a song and the work seems easier.

Every time I talk about this, someone calls out from the audience that "work isn't fun," that "there is a time and place for everything," or that this is somehow "coddling children." I don't agree with the premise that pain and gain are linked. The pain-gain model works in the short term but sabotages many folks in the long run. Children need to view work and learning in the positive. If what they do is not fun, children will not be able to sustain the motivation needed for a lifetime of work and learning.

6. Value all the ways learning occurs and all the ways to be successful.

Learning can occur in all circumstances. As an adult in a child's life, our job is to facilitate the learning experience by shaping perspective and perception to accommodate new knowledge. When seen as a potential lesson, every experience contributes to growth.

REMEMBER, WIN-WIN STRATEGIES rely on a willingness to discover the "third way." Win-win takes time and effort, but the gains are immense. Think about it. What would the world be like if we were all able to operate as winners?

Notes

1. Stephen Covey, quoted in *Quotes and Quips* (Provo, UT: Covey Leadership Center, 1993), p. 73.

2. Ibid., p. 74.

3. Mahatma Gandhi, quoted in *Quotes and Quips* (Provo, UT: Covey Leadership Center, 1993), p. 73.

4. Alfie Kohn, quoted in *Quotes and Quips* (Provo, UT: Covey Leadership Center, 1993), p. 74.

5. L. Tobin, *What to Do with a Child Like This?* (Duluth, MN: Whole Person Associates, 1991), p. 9.

Foster Cooperation

INTERVIEWER: What is it like to work in a group?
JUSTIN (age 10): You have four brains.

— Alfie Kohn[1]

T he win-win principle, coupled with a willingness to cooperate with one another, can change our relationships with
each other and make this a cooperative world that allows for
shared decision making and equal opportunities for all. My
mentor and guide in this arena is Alfie Kohn. His research on
the effects of competition is profound and compelling.[2] His
work has helped me understand that competition is fostered
to the detriment of children. Because he believes our society is
being poisoned by how we relate to one another, he challenges all of us to let go of rewards, bribes, and other extrinsic
methods of shaping behavior.

Kohn's findings are the basis of my philosophy about cooperation and they have become the primary challenge in my
parenting style. Like most parents, I fell into the quick fix of
bribing for good behavior. It works in the short run, but all of
us who have used extrinsic rewards know that we are creating children who come to expect some external reward for all
that they do. This is a difficult lesson to undo. Stuck in this
dilemma, I understand why Alfie Kohn titled his most recent
study *Punished by Rewards.*

In *No Contest: The Case Against Competition*, Alfie Kohn re-
views numerous studies and includes among the benefits of

cooperation "a surprising but equally consequential finding: when we cooperate, we are inclined to like each other more."[3] Kohn summarizes these studies and the clear benefits to children who are taught to cooperate rather than to compete.[4] In a cooperative environment, children:

- Are more likely to encourage each other.
- Are more sensitive to the needs of others.
- Are less self-centered and more easily see another's point of view.
- Have enhanced communication skills.
- Develop a greater sense of trust.

How does this relate to your children? All children need to learn how to be their best, assume responsibility, and work on a team. Cooperation brings people together, challenging them to combine their efforts for mutual benefit. Cooperation is a catalyst for effectiveness and shared responsibility. Extraordinary accomplishments are a likely product of teamwork.

Cooperation also fosters creativity. Teresa Amabile found that children asked to create artwork in a competitive event were far less creative, less varied, and less spontaneous than those allowed to create for personal pleasure.[5] Creative cooperation helps people do things in ways they hadn't contemplated before. Such self-discoveries are often experienced in cooperative settings.

The ability to work well with others, considered a valuable asset in the workplace, is highly recommended in the studies that analyze skill-building needs for the next century.[6] In one study, employers cite an inability to work with others as the main cause of employment termination. Yet parents and educators continue to place a higher value on competition than cooperation. Children are being encouraged to compete at younger and younger ages.

I am the lone mom in my neighborhood who has not signed up my daughter for soccer. Other parents have tried to convince me that soccer is not competitive, yet when we go to the games, I hear parents yelling "Get 'em!" There is no way that "Get 'em" can be interpreted as a positive, cooperative gesture. In fact, the experience of competition may be the reason children have become so motivated by extrinsic rewards.

Edward Deci and Richard Ryan found that motivation for extrinsic rewards (like winning the game or the contest) dramatically reduces enjoyment.[7] Perhaps this is why by age 15 most kids choose not to participate in team sports. This externalization of motivation may also be a contributing factor to many of the social problems we are facing today.

Children are not born competitive. According to Thomas Tutko and William Bruns,

> *Competition is a learned phenomenon.... people are not born with a motivation to win or to be competitive. We inherit a potential for a degree of activity, and we all have the instinct to survive. But the will to win comes through training and the influences of one's family and environment.*[8]

Many times I have said similar words to parents and teachers, only to hear the inevitable objection: "But competition is the way of the world." Competition *is* the way of the world, and it has truly caused us — and our children — more trouble and pain than almost any other social pattern.

For many, winning is the only pleasure life offers. These folks too often burden children with expectations that ignore the children's gifts and abilities, thereby setting them up for failure. This severely limits the range of experiences children can draw upon to make sense of their world.

As adults who want to teach cooperation to our children, we need to examine our own behavior. I have created a list of questions to help you determine if you use competition in your relationships. The inventory can also help you gauge your own competitiveness.

1. Do you compare your children with each other or with other children?

One girl I know stopped trying to achieve academically in the third grade — right after she overheard her mom tell a friend that the girl would never be as good a student as her brother. Only after ten years of pain was the girl able to confront her mom and tell her how much the comparison hurt.

2. Do you feel bad when your children don't do as well as you want them to?

I once counseled a woman whose presenting problem was that her children did not meet her expectations. She lamented her "condition" over and over, alleging that after all she had done for her children they *should* be what she wanted them to be. When I asked if she thought her attitude might affect the children, she retorted that her selfish brats never notice her. I contradicted her and assured her that they do notice.

3. Do you cheer when the other team fails?

At a local high school, two children were nearly killed when a brawl followed a high school football game. Many kids were hurt and both teams became ineligible to play football in their division. Many of the players' parents loudly protested the ineligibility status, an act that showed me that to these parents competition is more important than human interaction. A TV commentator overheard one child in a high school basketball tournament say, "It's great to beat her." The announcer commented that perhaps this competitor had lost the fun aspects of the sport.

4. Do you devalue others?

I once planned a classroom lesson with a teacher who reported she had two kids who were disposable. They wouldn't ever get "it." When I confronted her, she told me that I was idealistic and simple-minded if I thought all kids could learn. She did not convince me. All children deserve someone who believes they can DO and DO well.

5. Do you encourage children to win instead of play?

On the sideline of a football game, one dad confided that he was pushing his son to excel in the sport so that he would be eligible for a college scholarship. This same man also didn't understand why the coach repeatedly admonished his son for rough play. I think it was inevitable.

6. Do you have concern with only the outcome while ignoring the process?

Tanya Harding embodied this phenomenon, as she was implicated in the attack on Nancy Kerrigan with the hope of enhancing her own chances of qualifying for the 1994 Olympic Games. In a more down-to-earth example, one mom came to me before school to get her son's speller. She let me know confidentially that this was how she "helped" her son stay ahead of classmates. I didn't give her the speller. I have met numerous parents who believe that the end justifies the means. These are the same parents who get upset when their children are suspended from school for cheating on final exams.

EACH OF THESE SIX QUESTIONS, when answered "Yes," describes competition from varied points of view. While the process of competition is not necessarily harmful, people committed to winning often lose a sense of self and of others. They can become ruthless in their focus on outdoing others. Too often the result is a loss of conscience.

When I was a "baby" trainer (my third year as a trainer), I had accomplished well the tasks set before me. At contract time, I expected to get a raise. My boss said, "No raise. You are a great trainer, but a poor team player. Your job in this next year is to help others to be as good as you are." I had spent my entire professional life trying be better than anyone else. The rules were changing and I had to change too.

Two years ago, eight years after I was charged to become a team player, I lost my luggage on a business trip. The clothes were easy to replace, but I was left with no notes and no prepared outlines for my workshops. My colleagues came to my rescue. The majority of my notes were in their possession because I had shared.

I offer this as an example because I think adults are too quick to evaluate the behavior of children while ignoring their own attitudes and behaviors. Success in life relies on cooperation and respect. Together they engender self-esteem, enhanced achievement, social interaction, positive emotionality, and an increase in motivation. Cooperation and respect must be woven into the very fabric of how we live with children.

Many sociologists and psychologists have called the eighties "the ME generation." To make the nineties a "WE generation," we must shift from competition to cooperation. This shift is a necessary prerequisite to the creation of a safer and more productive society.

If we are to emancipate ourselves from the burden of competition and embrace cooperation, a new covenant about how we work with others is necessary. I wrote the Covenant of Cooperation to provide guidelines for people who want to work together with cooperation and respect as their guiding lights. To do this well, take the time to appreciate all you can be.

The Covenant of Cooperation

We believe that all humankind has the potential to contribute to a greater good. This potential flourishes in the spirit of cooperation and mutual respect. For that reason, we are dedicated to this covenant and will hold the following principles to be self-evident:

1. Always be kind to others.
2. Strive to share everything you know.
3. Value the gifts of others as you appreciate your own gifts.
4. Play so everyone has fun, enjoying the children and your own child within.
5. Think about how you can make the world a better place to live.
6. Seek honorable advice.
7. Take time to think, reflect, and contemplate.
8. Judge yourself with gentleness; judge no one else.
9. Speak honestly about how you feel.
10. Focus on the good.
11. Hope.
12. Behave in a manner that respects your beliefs.

We can change. We can embrace cooperation. Begin simply — with an inventory of what you have to offer others. Be generous and well-meaning in your assessment of yourself. You can be your own best critic and your own most valuable resource. Cooperation requires both. Try these five steps to ensure that you get the best out of your cooperative ventures.

Four Steps to Shifting to Cooperation

1. Seek evidence that every child is contributing to the group.

Help each child to be a valued contributor. Make sure all children are included. Provide rules that make any activity fair. Ensure that each child has many ways to participate.

2. Ask that only meaningful work be done.

Kids need to feel empowered by what they do. Ask them to DO only what is clearly needed and what has some obvious value. I am always reminded of the child who once reported he knew his parents did not think much of him because all they ever asked him to do was take out the garbage.

3. Value the end product and put it to good use.

Proudly display all work. Use whatever kids create, always. Appreciate the jokes and the insights children share with you.

4. Reinforce the process of cooperation.

Engage your children in cooperative activities — wash the car together, make a photo album, bake a cake. Reinforce cooperation by reporting what you see and how you have interpreted the behavior. "I really like how well everyone is working together. Nice job sharing, guys." Honor the contribution of everyone involved. Encourage teachers who use cooperative learning in their classrooms.

MORE THAN A GROUP STRATEGY, cooperation is a way of viewing our responsibilities in life. Too often adversarial relationships are framed so we don't have to work with others, so we can view ourselves as superior and others as inferior. Cooperation fosters the best in people, allows for contributions from everybody, and creates abundant opportunities to celebrate. If I could teach only one thing, it would be that when we cooperate we get the best from everyone involved. It takes only one experience with a child who has been helped to understand through a cooperative group effort to convince the most skeptical adults.

Notes

1. Alfie Kohn, *No Contest: The Case Against Competition* (Boston: Houghton Mifflin, 1992 revised edition), p. 197.

2. Alfie Kohn's three major works: *Punished by Rewards: The Trouble with Gold Stars, Incentive Plans, A's, Praise, and Other Bribes* (Boston: Houghton Mifflin, 1993 hardcover and 1995 paperback); *No Contest: The Case Against Competition* (Boston: Houghton Mifflin, 1992); *The Brighter Side of Human Nature: Altruism and Empathy in Everyday Life* (New York: Basic Books, 1992).

3. Alfie Kohn, *No Contest: The Case Against Competition* (Boston: Houghton Mifflin, 1992 revised edition), p. 149.

4. Ibid., p. 149–50.

5. Teresa M. Amabile. *The Motivation to Be Creative* (Buffalo: Bearly, 1987), p. 576.

6. United States Department of Labor, Secretary's Commission on Achieving Necessary Skills (SCANS), "What Work Requires of Schools: A SCANS Report for America 2000" (Washington, D.C.: United States Department of Labor, 1991).

7. Edward Deci and Richard Ryan, *Intrinsic Motivation and Self-determination in Human Behavior* (New York: Plenum, 1985), p. 82–83.

8. Thomas Tutko and William Bruns, *Winning Is Everything and Other American Myths* (New York: Macmillan, 1976), p. 53.

Eliminate Judgments, Create Possibilities

If you judge people, you have no time to love them.
— Mother Teresa[1]

I n the years I've worked with kids, I have seen an incredible amount of pain produced from judgments. Kids reel from off-the-cuff comments about their inability to do something, their stupidity, even their ugliness. If I could eliminate one experience from every child's life, it would be the experience of being judged.

Judgment is too often a disguised put-down couched as an opinion. The disguise doesn't fool kids, who unfortunately don't realize how damaging put-downs are to self-esteem. Adults need to learn to avoid judgment and use other methods of dealing with kids, ideas, or situations that are determined to be "bad."

Create possibilities for achievement by removing constraints. Create hope by setting up the child for success. Create opportunities by pointing the way to other possibilities. Can you imagine a generation of kids raised on creativity rather than judgment and guilt? I can.

Do any of these statements sound familiar?

- I hate his hair. He only prefers it that way to make me crazy.

- His teacher made him lose interest in school.

- My husband just doesn't care anymore. If he cared he would have remembered our anniversary.
- She has everything, yet all she ever does is complain.
- He is so bad even his own mother doesn't like him.
- She is a walking, talking busybody. Don't tell her any secrets.

Each of these statements reflects a judgment. Notice the formula:

1. Somebody guesses or assumes . . . then labels.
2. The judgment becomes a fact.
3. The fact becomes a truth.
4. The truth becomes the reality used to relate to the person who is judged.

Judgment never takes into account who people are or what kind of a day they are having. Being judged seldom feels good (unless you are winning), and if you feel *good* someone else probably feels *bad*. The following scenario further underscores what happens when judgment visits children.

> Aaron was a real troublemaker at school. He was angry most of the time and rude to other kids and the teachers. He was eventually expelled from school for repeatedly getting into fist fights.
>
> Aaron's younger brother, Jacob, entered the same junior high school the following year. During lunch on the first day of school, three teachers commiserated with each other about having another one of "them" in the school. Odds were jokingly taken about how long it would be before Jacob got into major trouble.
>
> That afternoon, there was a fight in the hallway during passing time. Two teachers intervened. The kids

who were watching scattered so fast the teachers were
unable to identify the two who had thrown the punches.
The principal asked the intervening teachers to identify the
kids who were involved. Five names were turned in.
Jacob's name was on the list, yet he had left the campus
before lunch to go to the dentist with his mom. He wasn't
even at school when the fight broke out.

Judgment, assumptions, and criticism are not conducive
to positive human interaction. An unhappy memory, social
reluctance, pessimism, and withdrawal are often the products
of an unwarranted judgment. Judgment usually leaves a mark
and can be very destructive.

Be honest. Those who judge, gossip, and assume the
worst are making themselves feel superior. These acts — ex-
tensions of competition — represent the ugly side of human
nature that wants others to look bad so we can seem better.

To break out of the judging pattern, replace your judgment with an unconditional acceptance that we are all unique
and will respond to the world in our own individual manner.
By no means does this require that you like everybody or that
you socialize with everybody. Acceptance merely disallows
judgment — good or bad.

It's hard to give up judging others if you have no dis-
cernible idea of how you might otherwise behave. Some positive options might include:

- Taking the time for self-reflection.
- Reading the words of others.
- Comparing religions, philosophies, and beliefs.
- Studying character portrayals of noted individuals of the
  past and present.
- Talking to one who is different from you.

These strategies will help you expand your tolerance and help you become more flexible. However, being nonjudgmental in theory and in practice are often very different. Making this DOism applicable to your relationships with children is a challenge. The following suggestions should help.

Three Steps to Eliminating Judgment

1. Think before you speak.

Take the time to carefully choose your words.

> BAD: You did this to hurt me.

> BETTER: My feelings are hurt.

> BEST: I haven't known what to think about what happened. I'm scared and my feelings are hurt. Regardless, I think we'll survive this.

2. Speak to the judgment.

Tell the child what you have assumed, opined, or judged.

> BAD: I know you intended to cheat.

> BETTER: I can only assume you intended to cheat.

> BEST: My first assumption is that you planned to cheat. My evidence of this is the cheat-sheet your teacher confiscated from your pocket. I assume you understand there will be consequences for your behavior. Cheating violates a major rule in our family.

3. Give voice to your process.

Let the child know what you are thinking.

> BAD: You are grounded. When your dad gets home, he'll decide how to punish you.

BETTER: I am very confused about this. I can't fathom how you made this choice.

BEST: I really need some time to think about what has happened. My first reaction is to punish you. I need to figure out what would be helpful. I'm worried, but I know that we'll work this out.

NOTICE THAT EACH SUGGESTION is tailored to the adult not the child. As adults, we have a responsibility to remain calm and in control. If we lose control, we need to report that as a fact and blame no one. You might say, "I can't handle this. I need a time-out just to know how I want to respond."

Don't assume that you will manage these suggestions just because you read this book. It takes time, practice, and more practice. The best plan is to develop short-term goals. Take a minute to name a goal and then list three of your special talents or skills that will help you achieve it. For example:

GOAL: Remove the things that get in the way of my relationship with my daughter.

1. Take some time off from work.

2. Spend more time doing things that interest both of us.

3. Plan a weekly good-time event that will create opportunities for supporting our relationship.

Can you imagine how your world would change if you used your energy in this fashion? Most of us could renew relationships, develop new dimensions to our lives, and start whole new lines of inquiry. The key to successfully shifting from the judgment of others to the ability to create new possibilities relies on your capacity to concentrate on yourself and your potential. Remember, whatever you focus on will expand!

Four Steps to Creating Possibilities

1. Remove constraints that have limited you in the past.

Carefully examine your constraints. Identify and eliminate those that are fraught with judgments. Look closely at your understanding of the current reality and examine your past in terms of how your own judgments have worked against you.

2. Be open to seeing the world from another's perspective.

I once advised a group of college students to read aloud what they had written. I assured them that this method would help them catch grammar errors, syntax problems, and faulty logic. I then listened as many of the students read their themes aloud. They failed to hear the errors! I learned that not everyone processes in similar ways. You can never assume that you know or can predict another's experience. Only through common, shared exploration can another person's perspective be known. We could all benefit from saying the Sioux Indian Prayer:

> *Great Spirit, help me never to judge another until I have walked in his moccasins.*[2]

3. Push yourself beyond the limits of your past.

As adults, we often limit the children in our lives rather than create possibilities for them. I have worked with many parents who assume their children will accomplish only what they were able to achieve. They don't encourage their children to break out of their mold. This process is called *delimitating* —

assuming limits because of our personal limits or experience. Comments like the following are indications of delimitations:

- Don't expect to do well in math. Your dad can't add.
- Irish (or any other ethnicity) never do well in science.
- Our family isn't in the same class as they are. Don't expect to get invited to the party.
- You have never understood that won't happen for people like us.
- I can't imagine why you thought you could do that.

Our potential — as well as that of our children — is only limited by our perceptions and dreams. I believe that none of us will ever be given an idea or a dream without also being given the tools to make it real. This parallels a personal belief that everything happens for a reason. I have come to understand that I will always be able to handle, in some fashion, whatever happens.

4. Be your best; your children will model what they see.

Effective role models walk their talk; they are what they ask others to be. This is the greatest gift you can give to children. Be exactly what you ask them to be. If you want them to be studious, then you be a great student. If you want them to be effective with communication, then you be a competent communicator. If you want them to be a person capable of love, then you be a master at honoring your relationships.

BUYING INTO YOUR RESPONSIBILITY as an adult in children's lives is demanding, exacting, and sometimes painful. Constant vigilance is necessary to check for congruency, consistency, and alignment. Adults tend to resist having to check themselves. We tend to have an unspoken, unconscious belief that as adults we should be exempt from having to constantly examine and monitor ourselves.

Given that DOism 7 is difficult, can you (will you) take the necessary time to carefully evaluate your relationships with children? Are you willing to create opportunities for the children in your life instead of judging them and wishing they were different? Creating, wishing, dreaming, and hoping for the best for yourself and your children — it's within your scope and subject to your choice.

You see things that are and say, "Why?" But I dream things that never were and say, "Why not?"
— George Bernard Shaw[3]

Notes

1. Mother Teresa, quoted in *Quotes and Quips* (Provo, UT: Covey Leadership Center, 1993), p. 23.

2. Sioux Indian Prayer, quoted in *Courage to Change* (New York: Al-Anon Family Groups, 1992), p. 197.

3. George Bernard Shaw, quoted in *Quotes and Quips* (Provo, UT: Covey Leadership Center, 1993), p. 55.

Value Respect and Responsibility

The natural moral law...
c an be expressed in terms of two great values:
respect and responsibility.
These values constitute the core
of a universal, public morality.
— Thomas Lickona[1]

A proponent of character education, Thomas Lickona describes respect and responsibility as the "action side of morality," qualities of character that lead to future success. These values make morality a reality and personal safety more than a hope. Here's how Lickona defines these two values:

Respect. *Respect means showing regard for the worth of someone or something. It takes three major forms: respect for oneself, respect for other people, and respect for all forms of life and the environment that sustains them.*[2]

Responsibility. *Responsibility is an extension of respect. If we respect other people, we value them. If we value them, we feel a measure of responsibility for their welfare.*[3]

The challenge for all adults is to become an implement of prosocial morés. Role modeling is of utmost importance, as is the creation of opportunities for children to serve others. In addition, parents and teachers need to offer effective learning experiences and lessons that encourage moral reflection. *Perhaps the greatest task to be assumed by adults is the reconstitution of prosocial values in our society and the reeducation of our children.*

Universal morality. It comes as a daily surprise that we no longer seem to share one. I prefer to challenge people to the exploration and acceptance of common values rather than spend my time trying to explain why this hiatus has occurred. For our purposes, people need common morés in order to maintain safe and productive communities.

After the 1992 riots in Los Angeles, I was asked to work with kids who had been arrested for the first time. They had looted businesses during the height of the civil unrest that followed the announcement of the acquittal of the four police officers accused of beating Rodney King. Some of the kids admitted having participated in the looting. When I asked how they made that choice, many reported that their parents had told them to go. They offered a number of justifications for this behavior:

- "The stores have insurance."
- "Everybody was doing it."
- "Looting is expected during a riot."
- "The people we stole from were probably bad people."
- "We needed the stuff more than the store owners."
- "It doesn't matter. This was a special thing."
- "I didn't hurt anybody, so it was cool."

As I challenged these perspectives, I found that most of the kids not only believed what they were saying, but created evidence to support their bias. It is too easy to say this was a product of cultural diversity and economic deprivation. The more we talked, the more I understood that the dilemma was moral rather than economic and cultural. The issue was one of character, not social class, color, or ethnicity.

Just when our social needs cry out for a universal morality, we no longer have one. Proponents of character education are not asking that everyone be the same, only that everyone accept the moral values of respect and responsibility: to be respectful of ourselves and of one another and to be responsible for the welfare of ourselves and others. I need to clarify.

Respect for Self

Respect for self mirrors a positive belief in one's personal capacity to handle circumstances in prosocial ways. Two distinct elements are components of self-respect: *positive* and *prosocial.* I have met many "gang" kids who have positive beliefs about themselves, yet they are antisocial in their behavior. In this context, they lack self-respect.

Having confidence in one's personal capabilities is evidence of self-respect. This is initially gained through positive interactions with meaningful adults. It is also a product of how we examine our experience and personal challenges.

Peer interactions become a primary source of feedback in early adolescence. For children who are not well-grounded — in a sense of themselves and who they want to be — adolescence can be dangerous. Dangerous? Yes. Without a respect for self, adolescents too often make decisions to follow the crowd. They commit immoral acts to gain peer acceptance and for the sheer exhilaration of breaking rules.

A child who has a prosocial sense of self (self-respect) is less likely to be influenced by peers. Those with positive and prosocial self-respect place high value on the *who* and the *how* of their lives. Self-respecting adolescents don't puke up their guts on the street, get caught in brawls, or commit acts of vandalism. A lack of self-respect is evident in drug abuse, promiscuous sex, chronic lying and cheating, and self-degradation.

Respect for Others

A basic foundation of a democratic society, respect for others is something we should all exemplify and openly espouse. It is portrayed in terms of recognition, acceptance, empathy, and kindness. Respect for others does not require agreement or shared experiences. Racism, prejudice, and crimes against people or property indicate a rejection of social morés and values, as well as a disregard for others.

Responsibility

When we ask others to be responsible, we are asking them to respond to a given task, situation, or dilemma. When we declare that others are responsible, we have determined that it is their duty to respond. Responsibility, then, carries with it a sense of commitment: We must DO for ourselves, and for others, in a *respectful* manner.

TOGETHER, RESPECT AND RESPONSIBILITY become catalysts for prosocial behavior. They are complementary to one another and basic to a positive social morality. Respect and responsibility can become universal values if we embrace them as *our* values. We make it happen when we demonstrate respect to ourselves and others. We *must* be intolerant of excuses and alibis that have allowed an acceptance of disrespect and a lack of responsibility. Please help in this process.

Five Steps to Teaching Respect and Responsibility

1. Provide children with clear messages about how you expect them to value self and others. Speak clearly and use the child's name.

ADULT TO CHILD

"Isaac, when you talk about others, be sure to say only things you would say *to* them."

"Melanie, I worry about you when you choose to describe yourself as 'stupid.' I need to understand what happened to make you say that about yourself."

ADULT TO ADOLESCENT

"Eli, your language is not acceptable. I need you to think about what you are saying and how you are speaking of others. I need evidence that you value others."

"Whoa! Did you hear what you just said? Cool it, Eric. Speaking about others that way is unacceptable in this house [classroom, neighborhood]."

2. Tell children how you have come to understand the role respect plays in your life. Demonstrate how you are respectful.

ADULT TO CHILD

"Look, Joseph. Sometimes it's hard to talk kindly to someone who is hurting your feelings."

"Carole, why do you suppose that being helpful is so important to me?"

ADULT TO ADOLESCENT

"Margaret, do you believe that what you did was the right way to handle this situation? I think that someone got hurt in this process."

"What's going on? That was not cool, José. I was appalled when I saw what you did. Can you understand this?"

3. Give responsibility to children. Allow children to choose the ways they want to be responsible.

ADULT TO CHILD who has said, "I need some help."

"Do you think you could do this with me, Lisa?"

"Alex, what do you need to be able to do this?"

"Alicia, help me know what you want your contribution to be."

ADULT TO ADOLESCENT who has said, "I need some help."

"Nancy, from all that needs to be done, what do you see that you could learn from doing?"

"I really believe that you are capable of helping more with the chores of running the house. I need your help, Wayne."

"Shirley, take seriously everything you do. Do it well and to the best of your ability."

4. Provide surprise rewards for responsible or respectful behavior, but commit to no bribes.

ADULT TO CHILD

"I have noticed that you play really well with Erika. I liked how you asked her opinion about how to play the game."

"Ryan, let's get some ice cream to celebrate working so hard in school. We deserve some time together."

"I love how well you have been taking care of your things, Megan, and I thought you deserved a new doll for your collection."

ADULT TO ADOLESCENT

"Hey, Eddy, do you have time to go practice your driving with me?"

"Your mom said you handled that situation at school really well, Julian. Let's go get some coffee at Café Roma. I'd love to hear about what happened."

"Thanks for taking care of your sister last night, Bart. I felt better knowing you were home and in charge."

5. Acknowledge extraordinary effort.

ADULT TO CHILD

"Cool, Sabrina. You really did a nice job taking care of your cousin. I love to watch you helping younger kids."

"Michael, that was great!"

"You are the best, Abe. I think you make the world a better place!"

ADULT TO ADOLESCENT

"Jeremy, you win the award for the neatest kid in this neighborhood! I love how willing you were to jump in and help."

"Nice job, Kathy. I'm always amazed at how well you do with others. I'm proud to be related to you."

EACH OF THESE FIVE STEPS creates opportunities to affirm and positively reflect upon the behavior of a child, young or old. The power of positive reflection must be experienced. This process cannot be cognitively framed. Kids need to see, hear, and feel your approval. Kids (and all living things, I suspect) need to be nurtured with kindness and valid behavioral feedback. But hear this: Tough feedback should only be given when the relationship is positive.

Look at your relationship if a child has difficulty hearing what you say. Probably you are not a legitimate source of feedback in the child's opinion. Legitimacy is determined by how the child has (or has not) given you influence over his or her life. You can only teach those who have given you legitimate influence to take on such a task. The quality of your relationship is reflected in how the child receives critical feedback.

DOism 1, speaking to the positive, helps build the kind of relationships that can serve the child through any experience of adversity, trauma, or pain. With consistent and abundant use of DOism 1, relationships can be built in which everyone can be heard, valued, and helped. In the end, respect and responsibility must become an integral part of how you really manage your life. You can't fake it either; kids always smell phonies. Be real, be positive, accept responsibility, and respect others. Your children will then follow in your footsteps.

Notes

1. Thomas Lickona, *Educating for Character: How Our Schools Can Teach Respect and Responsibility* (New York: Bantam, 1992), p. 43.

2. Ibid., p. 43.

3. Ibid., p. 44.

Learn to Say Yes

Say "Yes" and then figure out how to make it work.
— Wayne Hunnicutt[1]

Saying YES jump-starts a relationship, structuring what will happen in terms that are positive and that foster hope. Learning to say YES is a complement to DOism 1, Sort to the Positive. While grounded in an affirmative perspective, saying YES asks for another aspect of interaction. It empowers children while keeping adults involved in their lives. This DOism can change the very nature of your relationships with children.

Stephen Glenn, the author of several books on child advocacy, once said something like "...kids have only ten minutes a day with adults when they are not being ordered, directed and commanded."[2] I first heard these words at a conference many years ago. I remember being introduced to the ideas of Stephen Glenn at a moment that made a significant difference in my life. Think about it. How often is your exchange with a child something other than "No," "Don't," "Stop," or "Why didn't you...?"

Kids need to be embraced with positives. Carl Rogers called it unconditional positive regard.[3] Urie Bronfenbrenner talked about it as irrational loving.[4] Today's kids call it "being way cool." Saying YES allows for an acceptance of a desired outcome, but stipulates the boundaries that must exist for the YES to be honored.

Mom, can I go to the store with Billy?
YES, if Billy's mom is going.

Mrs. Karns, may I turn in my term paper on Friday?
YES, if you add an extra three pages to the length of the paper.

Dad, can I go skiing with friends?
YES, if I meet the adult chaperone before the trip.

See how easy it is to say YES? The entire interaction is altered because YES provides hope and the potential for negotiation. It also frames the interaction in terms of what is possible, rather than what is not.

Empowerment never occurs when the adult maintains all the control. Telling children what to DO is usually met with resistance. Helping them discover what needs to be done, or can be done, shifts the focus of the dialogue. This allows the adult to set up conditions that keep the kids safe while allowing *them* to choose what to DO. Some say this is manipulation. I prefer to think of it as benign manipulation. We are manipulating to create boundaries, safety, and protective conditions — which is our job as adults.

Too many of our kids' interactions with adults begin with "Can I...?" and end with the adult saying "No." What do you suspect an ongoing barrage of NOs does to a relationship? Every child responds differently, but respond they do nonetheless. When NOs predominate, kids are likely to stop asking for permission and start creating runarounds so they can DO what they want without permission. I suspect this becomes the first stage of their rebellion against the adults in their lives.

Learning to say YES teaches compromise, contracting, and cooperation. I would much prefer that we take the time to learn to say YES than try to manage the difficulties engendered by the loss of boundaries and adults in a child's life.

Many adults reading this book are already familiar with some of the common consequences of too many NOs:

1. The adult becomes distrustful of solicitations for permission.

2. The child fails to learn valuable communication skills, including the art of negotiation.

3. The adult misses opportunities to listen to a child's wants and desires.

4. The child begins to doubt how things can work out in his or her favor, which in turn often cultivates a sense that nothing the child does or wants is valid.

5. The adult is forced to assume an inappropriate role as permission-giver, while the adult should be viewed as a boundary-keeper and safety-maker.

THE VALIDITY OF THIS DOISM is based on the acceptance of three basic assumptions that reflect my personal and professional experience:

1. All kids want approval from adults.

2. All kids want structure.

3. All kids want to feel in control.

For this DOism to work, *you must mean what you say.* The child must know that it's acceptable to request permission. Once the parameters you set are met, the child must get to DO what was asked. Many times I have seen adults renege on agreements, which is absolutely unacceptable. Not keeping your word defies all that the process of YES implies — important things like trust, respect, and cooperation.

Many adults who first try this DOism sabotage the essence of the YES message by the tone of voice used. Pay attention to both what you say and how you say it. Try to impose these simple conditions on any request:

- Do I understand what is desired?
- Am I clear about what will happen, who will be there, where they will be, and what they will be doing?
- Is the request legal, moral, and otherwise acceptable?
- Do I agree with the plan, activity, or event?
- Is this agreement consistent with my beliefs?

Each of these questions is designed to help you be "in the know." Take all the time you need to clearly understand the request. If you can answer all these questions in the affirmative, say YES. For any of these questions you cannot answer in the affirmative, restate the question until you are clear that you are "in the know." It's easy to make assumptions and fail to get all the necessary information, especially if you give up on the process.

None of this will work until you have clearly established what is *not* negotiable. For example, can your child attend an unchaperoned party at age fourteen? At age eighteen? Is a little alcohol okay if your sixteen-year-old son isn't driving? Is marijuana okay? Many adults assume that the answers to questions like these are obvious. Never assume that your forty-year-old "obvious" is anything like a child's observations.

The younger the child is, the more you will have to provide creative options. To a teenager, instead of YES, you can say, "You can turn in the paper late if you write three more pages on the subject." To a younger child, you may need to say, "Yes, I understand that you are worried about getting your job done. Help me understand what's getting in the way of you getting this done." Then "Yes, I can agree to the delay under these circumstances...."

Besides improving your relationships with children, this DOism will model an example of how the children in your life might behave with others. You know you've been successful when you hear your daughter say to her younger sister, "YES, you may borrow my sweater for right now. I will need it back before school tomorrow morning."

Three Steps to Saying Yes

1. Develop a relationship with children that includes boundaries.

Boundaries must be clear and dynamic — that is, boundaries must change as the child is maturing. While it may be appropriate to tell a six-year-old that she can go to the store if an adult is present, the same message would be grossly inappropriate for a girl fourteen years old. The gradual expansion of boundaries requires that you have a clear sense of the ability and the developmental capability of the child. The best guide to developmental cues is the *child's* experience, not *your* experience. Assessing your child's reality by the circumstances of *your* past is a problem waiting to happen. Your experience in no way parallels their reality.

2. Value the child's requests as real and valid.

All requests must be viewed as real and valid. If a child asks for something that is clearly outrageous, acknowledge the request in an equally outrageous way. "Mom," says fourteen-year-old Susie, "get me some cigarettes at the store." "Sure," I might say, "as soon as you can convince me that smoking is a healthy pastime." All requests must be acknowledged and then framed by the conditions that will make YES possible. The key here is not to use put-downs.

3. Seriously consider the outcome you desire.

This is the most difficult step. For example, if you say YES and require that contact be made with someone, then you need to do the follow-up. Nothing is worse for a child than an adult who sets limits or stipulations that are not honored by the adult. This need happen only once to communicate a double message. Whenever a double message is used, children are then left to their own devices.

SAYING YES STARTS ANY DIALOG in the positive and structures the dimensions of the compromises. Saying YES shares control, gives choices, and makes children's goals achievable. Saying YES changes possibilities for your children from "why I can't" to "how I can." Saying YES will help you realize that abundance can be everyone's life experience. When the sky is the limit, anything becomes possible.

Notes

1. Wayne Hunnicutt, Chief Executive Officer, National Training Associates, at a 1989 marketing meeting.
2. Stephen H. Glenn and Jane Nelsen, *Raising Self-Reliant Children in a Self-Indulgent World: Seven Building Blocks for Developing Capable Young People* (Rocklin, CA: Prima, 1989).
3. Carl Rogers, *On Becoming a Person* (Boston: Houghton Mifflin, 1972).
4. Urie Bronfenbrenner, *The Ecology of Human Development: Experiments by Nature and Design* (Cambridge, MA: Harvard, 1979).

Use Humor and Laughter

Humor is one of the truly elegant defenses
in the human repertoire.
Few would deny that the capacity for humor,
like hope, is one of mankind's most potent antidotes
for the woes of Pandora's box.
— George Valiant[1]

To embrace children with humor is to embrace them with a language they can readily understand. Laughter heals, serves as a natural high, and fosters hope. Laughter provides a release — both physical and emotional. It is a coping strategy that can lead to intimacy. As the Danish pianist and humorist Victor Borge said, "Humor is the shortest distance between two people."[2]

Humor adds more excitement to life experience and is a superb method for coping and reducing stress. Humor creates energy and attracts others. A shared experience honed by humor is unparalleled and remembered as unique. A great belly laugh provides the same biochemical "rush" as many illicit drugs. The difference is that laughter is a healthy product of human interaction. It is always available and never responds to the laws of supply and demand.

Something is very attractive about good laughers. They draw people to them and make human connections exciting.

Where laughter is prevalent, life is more fun. Most people who have survived great adversity have a highly developed sense of humor. For them, humor has become a resource to manage difficulty. It can become the means to move from the source of difficulty to one aimed at a solution.

In DOism 1, I mentioned humor as integral to sorting to the positive. Because laughter is the single most enriching experience of my life, it deserves a DOism of its own. I love to laugh. I like it even better when I can help others laugh. Laughter makes for the best memories. Somewhere along my life path, I learned that laughter lightens burdens and brings people closer together. People who laugh are attractive, inviting, and more relaxed. Because I wanted to BE those things, I had to learn to laugh.

If you watch them, you'll notice that great laughers laugh at themselves and their particular circumstances. They never laugh at someone else's expense. There is an important difference between laughter and ridicule. Ridicule hurts. Humor heals. The distinction between laughter and ridicule must be recognized. (See Table 10.1 on page 101.)

One way to ensure that you don't breach the boundaries between humor and ridicule is to speak only of your own experiences. Be the center of your own jokes, but pay attention to the fine line between speaking about yourself and self-degradation. Degradation — whether of others or yourself — is never a good vehicle for humor.

The benefits of laughter are many. Laughter reduces stress and bridges gaps. Laughter is a shared, warming experience. Learning is enhanced with laughter. Great laughers tend to let go of the past. They understand that how they view their circumstances makes a difference. I think somewhere along the line they had to make a choice to laugh or cry. Their choice may have been a matter of survival with humor used to heal.

Table 10.1 Humor Versus Ridicule[3]

Laughing WITH	Laughing AT
Going for the jocular vein	Going for the jugular vein
Based on caring and empathy	Based on contempt and insensitivity
Builds confidence	Destroys confidence through put-downs
Involves people in the fun	Excludes some people
A person makes a choice to be the butt of a joke (as in "laughing at yourself")	A person does not have a choice in being made the butt of a joke
Amusing — invites people to laugh	Abusing — offends people
Supportive	Sarcastic
Brings people closer	Divides people
Leads to positive repartee	Leads to one-downmanship cycle
Pokes fun at universal foibles	Reinforces stereotypes by singling out a particular group as the butt of a joke

Laughter can become protective armor. Perspective and mind-sets make laughter possible even in the face of pain. The best laughers like to see the irony in situations. They like to make everything into a story. As a story, the often bizarre circumstances become insightful, instructional, and relationship building.

Humor and laughter are not given to you; they are learned skills refined by the life experiences that are uniquely yours. Your perspective will frame your personal brand of humor. You deserve to enjoy it. With a willingness to view life in simple terms and to recognize the absurd, anyone can learn to DO humor. DOism 10 can be woven into all your interactions with children. Kids are attracted to laughter and want to be with laughers. Take the next five steps to make humor a reality in your life.

Five Steps to the Effective Use of Humor and Laughter

1. Keep it simple.

The simpler the situation the more likely kids will be able to see the humor. Simple humor involves three specific dimensions: outrageous physical ploys, surprise, and absurdity. Kids love the humor created in silly physical terms like those portrayed in the *Home Alone* movies and TV's *America's Home Videos*. Kids love to laugh with people, but they hate being laughed at so be sure they're not the butt of your jokes.

2. Notice and appreciate the absurd.

There are opportunities to laugh every moment of every day. My daughter often gets dressed with me. I'll "forget" to put on my pants and then pretend to be headed outside. She'll screech that I am forgetting something important. I blush, she laughs. It's a great way to start the day and she never tires of it. I also love to catch people doing funny things when they think no one is looking. Cars seem to be the best place to find people making faces, practicing singing, or doing the bee bop boogie. My daughter and I make a game of it all the time; we call it the Catch People Unaware contest. When you look you'll see funny things all around you.

3. Take yourself more lightly.

When she was three, my daughter wore the same dress to preschool for five months straight. She loved the pink frilly dress that made her feel beautiful. Her father and I kept threatening her with dire consequences because she would wear only her pink dress. Finally, after much stress, tears, and arguments, I let go and told her to wear her dress. It was my problem, not hers. Shortly thereafter, she no longer wanted to wear the pink frock. We still laugh about it. Make sure that your child-centered problems are not merely a product of your embarrassment, judgment, or preconceived "rights."

4. Talk only about real experiences.

Share what really happened and why it was humorous to you. Don't lie to make something funny. The more true-to-life the story, the funnier it is. When I was a new therapist, I once told my supervisor that a client had "decomposed" in my office. (I should have said "decompensated.") My supervisor responded with a strained "Really?" This is a great story to share with counselors and psychologists.

5. Talk only about shared circumstances.

Whenever you use humor, be clear that an age-appropriate linkage can be made. Unless you share a common reality, others may not understand or appreciate what is being said. Menopausal hot flashes are not appropriate fodder for humor with third-grade children, but word play and just plain silly stories are good for children of all ages.

LIFE IS MUCH MORE FUN if you don't take it too seriously. Humor and laughter can be incorporated into every aspect of your experiences with children. You can create an environment full of opportunities for laughter. You can view your experiences through the lens of humor. Laugh and you'll reduce stress, have more fun, and be more attractive to others! What do you have to lose?

Notes

1. George E. Valiant, *Adaptation to Life* (Boston: Little, Brown, 1973), quoted in Herbert Benson and Eileen M. Stuart, *The Wellness Book: The Comprehensive Guide to Maintaining Health and Treating Stress-Related Illness* (New York: Simon & Schuster, 1992), p. 266.

2. Victor Borge, quoted in Herbert Benson and Ellen M. Stuart, *The Wellness Book: The Comprehensive Guide to Maintaining Health and Treating Stress-Related Illness* (New York: Simon & Schuster, 1992), p. 267.

3. Dr. Joel Goodman, ed., *Laughing Matters*, volume 5, number 2 (Saratoga Springs, NY: The Humor Project, Inc.). Reprinted with permission. For a free information packet on the positive power of humor, send a stamped ($1) self-addressed envelope to The Humor Project, Inc., Dept. NTA, 110 Spring Street, Saratoga Springs, NY 12866, or call (518) 587-8770. This table is also reprinted in *The Wellness Book: The Comprehensive Guide to Maintaining Health and Treating Stress-Related Illness* by Herbert Benson and Eileen M. Stuart (New York: Simon & Schuster, 1992).

The Challenge

Everyone has his own specific vocation or mission in life....
Therein he cannot be replaced, nor can his life be repeated.
Thus, everyone's task is as unique
as is his specific opportunity to implement it.
— Viktor Frankl[1]

Integrating the DOisms into your daily life will help you develop the connections, the capacity, and the convictions to create the kind of future you want. The DOisms are not commandments to be followed; they are strategies that work to make quality relationships a reality. Reading about the DOisms is far easier than DOing them and DOing them consistently. Don't try to DO all ten at once.

For most people, the DOisms require a change in perception. Negative to positive. Rigid to flexible. Past-focused to future-focused. Lose to win. Failure to feedback. Competition to cooperation. Anger to laughter. Commands to internal values. NO to YES. Distance to trust.

Changing perception is difficult. Phase in the DOisms one at a time. As with most skills and strategies, accomplishment takes practice. Don't expect perfection; expect and strive for progress. The DOisms are effective only if you get to the point where you can apply them *and* experience the benefit of your efforts.

Seven discrete tasks will help foster the integration of the DOisms:

1. Look at the whole of what you do.

Pay attention to the entire picture, the movie of your life. Don't analyze the frames. Analysis of isolated moments often leads to poor generalizations and negativity.

2. Focus on the processes.

Every interaction, every connection you make can create a memory and provides an opportunity for you to "dance" in your relationship. Focus on the dance, not the steps. Enjoy the fluidity and rhythms that can be heard and experienced when you dance. Celebrate the rapport you create.

3. Value the sensitive and evolving nature of all your relationships.

Hope and desire drives most of us. Appreciate the emotional dimension of your experiences; it is truly what connects us all, always. Caring relationships are based on a commitment to the three L's: listening, learning, and loving.

> *Listening* is evidence of your interest in what is said. It confirms experience and makes real the possibility of help. We have one mouth and two ears. I suspect this is not a mistake.

> *Learning* together brings people closer. It makes memories. Learning feeds the mind and nurtures the soul. All of us can enhance the quality of our lives by committing to a lifelong learning process. To do this requires an open mind, a desire to understand, and an ever-constant desire to be the best we can possibly be.

> *Loving* is evidence that you care. How you love reflects your best self. Love pulls people together and gives

promise for the future. When love is absent, so are hope and optimism. I know of no better way to define *love* than as a consuming desire for the good of others.

4. Recognize that all energy comes from the relationship.

Each relationship relies on a collision of invisible energy fields that are uniquely our own. When our energy collides, a new combined energy — the relationship — is created. The relationship is then fostered and shaped by the energy shared. If your experiences are negative, the relationship is negative. Positive begets positive.

5. Recognize the moral obligation of your core principles.

Values that prescribe a certain behavior or attitude require consistent adherence to the principles they uphold. For example, I believe all children deserve to be safe, so I behave, think, and feel in ways that are congruent with that core principle. I watch carefully when I am driving, I report dangerous circumstances, I cry when I hear gross abuse stories, and I work in both my private and professional life to keep children safe.

6. Provide meaningful opportunities for youth involvement in real-life work.

As a society, we have disconnected children from the fabric that should protect them. This has created a sub-society — children influenced by other children with too little adult guidance. We need a social system that re-invests in the children. Meaningful work, community service, and service learning (volunteer work that is linked to specified curricular issues) help connect kids to the community.

7. Build the skills necessary for accepting self-responsibility.

Three skills are vital to self-responsibility: reflection, planning, and evaluation. With these skills, children can take charge of their own responses to whatever comes their way.

WHEN ASSIMILATED, EACH OF THESE tasks will ultimately contribute to a healthy and safe community. Aren't our relationships with children meant to provide them with the tools to live and work in a future community? What is community, anyway? Is it essential to belong to a community? Is a community defined by physical boundaries? Does a community have to share a common purpose or mission? What do we need to DO to be part of a community?

I reflect upon my own upbringing to answer some of these questions. When I was a child, a high value was placed on capable children. Parents sacrificed many personal joys and monetary gains for the overall well-being of the family. Children were encouraged to help others, to respect the essence of democracy, to honor family, and — above all — to lead a moral life. Good and bad were clearly defined and reinforced. My neighborhood, church, school, family, and friends comprised my community. These social institutions bonded together to define morés, boundaries, and expectations.

Society has drastically changed. These social institutions no longer dominate the lives of our children. The school is often the only social institution to which children have ties.

Urban neighborhoods are often hostile to children. Many families no longer have membership in churches or any system that prescribes "good" behavior.

We cannot recreate what has been, nor do we want to, for it would not fit into today's world. However, we *can* create a community that will nurture our children and keep them safe. When I became a mom, I became more of a zealot about the quality of my community and of my family life. I quickly learned that I could not be exclusive and self-oriented about these issues. Given the chance and the right circumstances, all humans are self-righting. For evidence, you need only look at the way people rally together in times of crisis. Missing children. Firestorms. Floods. Tornadoes. Earthquakes. We can DO together what none of us can DO alone.

As a consultant, I work within schools and communities all over the United States. I continue to be awestruck by the number of people struggling to find answers to make the world a safer and better place for children. In the past, I mistakenly felt that these issues of children and community were uniquely urban and North American. They are not. There are caring people all over the world who are rallying to make changes to protect and serve children.

I want to be part of the movement that brings hope back into our neighborhoods and puts kids first. To make this vision a reality we must reconstitute a sense of community. We cannot remain so disaffiliated and achieve success.

If you have profound convictions that support a movement of this kind, you must be willing to face the difficult challenges and commit to achieving the necessary changes. If you are willing to *embrace* change, do so out of a heartfelt desire to make a difference. Change is always initiated by people who genuinely *feel* the need.

The DOisms will help to redesign your personal world,

but they are also tools for societal change. They reflect the essence of what needs to be done on your journey. Be prepared. You may have to travel alone for a while. The focus is not on changing our behavior, our outsides. We've been working on those for years. Now is the time for changes *within:* the way we *feel* about one another, the way we *think,* and the beliefs that frame how we *live.*

The DOisms reflect the actions and changes that will make a difference. They challenge us to be open in our relationships with children and to restore ways to connect our youth to a more hopeful future. Only with a sense of future will our children be able to commit to moral action. The DOisms give voice to a moral code that will bring us back together. Utilize these DOisms to become a caring guide to the future: one who understands that every interaction is a potential memory and lesson. Now go and DO for children. You are the one who can make the difference.

Note

1. Viktor Frankl, quoted in *Quotes and Quips* (Provo, UT: Covey Leadership Center, 1993), p. 48.

Bibliography

Amabile, Teresa M. *The Motivation to Be Creative*. Buffalo: Bleary, 1987.

———. "Children's Artistic Creativity: Detrimental Effects of Competition in a Field Setting." *Personality and Social Psychology Bulletin* 8 (1982): 573–78.

Armstrong, Thomas. *In Their Own Way*. Los Angeles: Tarcher Press, 1987.

Barker, Joel Arthur. *Paradigms: The Business of Discovering the Future*. New York: HarperBusiness, 1992.

———. *Future Edge: Discovering the New Paradigms of Success*. New York: William Morrow, 1992.

Bateson, Gregory. *Mind and Nature: A Necessary Unity*. New York: Bantam Books, 1988.

Benard, Bonnie. *Fostering Resiliency in Kids: Protective Factors in the Family, School and Community*. Portland: Western Regional Center for Drug Free Schools and Communities, Northwest Regional Educational Laboratory, 1991.

———. "Resiliency Paradigm Validates Craft Knowledge," *Western Center News*. Portland: Northwest Regional Educational Laboratory, September 1993.

Bennis, Warren, and Joan Goldsmith. *Learning to Lead: A Workbook on Becoming a Leader*. Reading, MA: Addison-Wesley, 1994.

Benson, Herbert, and Eileen M. Stuart. *The Wellness Book: The Comprehensive Guide to Maintaining Health and Treating Stress-Related Illness*. New York: Simon & Schuster, 1992.

Bronfenbrenner, Urie. *The Ecology of Human Development: Experiments by Nature and Design.* Harvard University Press, 1979.

Canfield, Jack, and Mark Hansen. *Chicken Soup for the Soul: One Hundred One Stories to Open the Heart and Rekindle the Spirit.* Dearfield Beach, FL: Health Communications, 1993.

Canfield, Jack, and Frank Siccone. *One Hundred One Ways to Develop Student Self-Esteem and Responsibility: The Teacher's Coach.* Needham Heights, MA: Allyn & Bacon, 1992.

Capra, Fitjof. *The Turning Point: Science, Society and the Rising Culture.* New York: Bantam Books, 1987.

——. *The Tao of Physics: An Exploration of the Parallels Between Modern Physics and Eastern Mysticism,* 3rd ed. Boston: Shambhala, 1991.

Covey, Stephen R. *Quotes and Quips.* Provo, UT: Covey Leadership Center, 1993.

——. *Principle-Centered Leadership: Strategies for Personal and Professional Effectiveness.* New York: Simon & Schuster, 1992.

——. *The Seven Habits of Highly Effective People.* New York: Simon & Schuster, 1989.

Covey, Stephen R., A. Roger Merrill, and Rebecca R. Merrill. *First Things First: A Principle-Centered Approach to Time and Life Management.* New York: Simon & Schuster, 1994.

Csikszentmihalyi, Mihaly. *Flow: The Psychology of Optimal Experience.* New York: HarperCollins, 1990.

Deci, Edward, and Richard Ryan. *Intrinsic Motivation and Self-determination in Human Behavior.* New York: Plenum, 1985.

dePree, Max. *Leadership Is an Art.* New York: Doubleday, 1989.

——. *Leadership Jazz.* New York: Doubleday, 1992.

Dinkmeyer, Don, and Gary D. McKay. *The Parent's Handbook: Systematic Training for Effective Parenting.* New York: Random, 1989.

——. *Parenting Teenagers: Systematic Training for Effective Parenting.* New York: Random, 1990.

——. *Systematic Training for Effective Teaching: Activities for Teachers and Students.* Circle Pines, MN: American Guidance Service, 1980.

Dreikurs, Rudolf. *The Challenge of Parenthood.* New York: NAL-Dutton, 1991.

Dreikurs, Rudolf, and Zuckerman, Lawrence. *Children: The Challenge.* New York: NAL-Dutton, 1991.

Drucker, Peter F. *Managing for the Future: The 1990s and Beyond.* New York: Dutton, 1992.

Durkheim, Emile. *Moral Education: A Study in the Theory and Application of the Sociology of Education.* New York: Free Press, 1973.

Fiske, Edward B. *Smart Schools, Smart Kids: Why Do Some Schools Work?* New York: Simon & Schuster, 1992.

Fritz, Robert. *The Path of Least Resistance: Learning to Become the Creative Force in Your Own Life.* New York: Fawcett-Columbine, 1989.

Fullan, Michael. *Change Forces: Probing the Depths of Educational Reform.* London: Falmer Press, 1993.

Gardner, Howard. *The Unschooled Mind: How Children Think and How Schools Should Teach.* New York: Basic Books, 1993.

Garmezy, Norman, and Michael Rutter. *Stress, Coping and Development in Children.* Baltimore: Johns Hopkins University Press, 1984.

Gibbs, Jeanne, and Sherrin Bennett. *Together We Can Reduce the Risks of Alcohol and Drug Use Among Youth.* Sausalito, CA: Interactive Learning Systems, 1990.

Glasser, William. *The Quality School,* 2nd ed. New York: HarperCollins, 1992.

Gleick, James. *Chaos: Making a New Science.* New York: Penguin Books, 1988.

Glenn, H. Stephen, and Jane Nelsen. *Raising Self-Reliant Children in a Self-Indulgent World: Seven Building Blocks for Developing Capable Young People.* Rocklin, CA: Prima, 1989.

Glickman, Carl. *Renewing America's Schools.* San Francisco: Jossey-Bass, 1993.

Goodman, Joel (ed.). *Laughing Matters.* Saratoga Springs, NY: The Humor Project, Inc.

Helmstetter, Shad. *What to Say When You Talk to Your Self.* New York: Simon & Schuster, 1986.

Kohn, Alfie. *The Brighter Side of Human Nature: Altruism and Empathy in Everyday Life.* New York: Basic Books, 1992.

———. *No Contest: The Case Against Competition.* New York: Houghton Mifflin, 1992.

———. *Punished by Rewards: The Trouble with Gold Stars, Incentive Plans, A's, Praise, and Other Bribes.* New York: Houghton Mifflin, 1993.

Land, George, and Beth Jarman. *Break-point and Beyond: Mastering the Future.* New York: HarperBusiness, 1992.

Lazear, David. *Seven Ways of Teaching: The Artistry of Teaching with Multiple Intelligences.* Palatine, IL: Skylight Publishing, 1991.

Lickona, Thomas. *Educating for Character, How Our Schools Can Teach Respect and Responsibility*. New York: Bantam Books, 1992.

McNally, David. *Even Eagles Need a Push: Learning to Soar in a Changing World*. New York: Delacorte Press, 1990.

Montagu, Ashley. *Darwin, Competition and Cooperation*. Westport, CN: Greenwood Press, 1973.

——. *Man and Aggression*, 2nd ed. New York: Oxford University Press, 1973.

Nelsen, Jane. *Positive Discipline A–Z*, rev. ed. Rocklin, CA: Prima, 1993.

——. *Positive Discipline in the Classroom: How to Effectively Use Class Meetings and Other Positive Discipline Strategies*. Rocklin, CA: Prima, 1993.

Nelsen, Jane, and Stephen H. Glenn. *Time Out: A Guide for Parents and Teachers Using Popular Discipline Methods to Empower and Encourage Children*. Fair Oaks, CA: Sunrise Press, 1992.

Nelsen, Jane, and Lynn Lott. *I'm on Your Side: Resolving Conflict with Your Teenage Son or Daugher*. Rocklin, CA: Prima, 1991.

Oakley, Ed, and Doug Krug. *Enlightened Leadership: Getting to the Heart of Change*. New York: Simon & Schuster, 1993.

Peat, David F. *Synchronicity*. New York: Bantam Books, 1987.

Piaget, Jean. *The Moral Judgment of the Child*. New York: Free Press, 1965.

Rogers, Carl. *On Becoming a Person*. Boston: Houghton Mifflin, 1972.

Selye, Hans. *The Stress of Life*, 2nd ed. New York: McGraw Hill, 1978.

Senge, Peter M., *The Fifth Discipline: The Art and Practice of the Learning Organization.* New York: Doubleday, 1990.

Spock, Benjamin M. *Better World for Our Children: Rebuilding American Family Values.* Bethesda, MD: National Press Books, 1994.

Stacey, Ralph D. *Managing the Unknowable: Strategic Boundaries Between Order and Chaos in Organizations.* San Francisco: Jossey-Bass, 1992.

Tutko, Thomas, and William Bruns. *Winning Is Everything and Other American Myths.* New York: Macmillan, 1976.

Werner, Emily, and Ruth Smith. *Overcoming the Odds: High Risk Children from Birth to Adulthood.* Ithaca, NY: Cornell University Press, 1992.

———. *Vulnerable But Invincible: A Longitudinal Study of Resilient Children and Youth.* New York: Adams, Bannister, and Cox, 1989.

Wheatley, Margaret. *Leadership and the New Science: Learning About Organization from an Orderly Universe.* San Francisco: Berrett-Koehler Publishers, 1992.

About the Author

Michelle Karns is a charismatic leader for educational change. Her passion is to help schools, communities, and families create caring environments for their children. She has traveled extensively throughout the United States pleading for greater understanding of the plight of children and suggesting ways that this may be accomplished.

Her many keynote addresses and conference presentations focus on increasing audience awareness of the reality experienced by today's children and on ways to build individual coping skills. She does this by reaching adults who have influence with kids and by interacting with the kids directly. She originated the popular Kids Day program, and has helped develop other programs that engender healthy relationships among kids, parents, and teachers.

All of Michelle's work reflects her commitment to making real the dream of kid-centered, community-supported, healthy school environments. With parents, she strives for more empathetic relationships. With school staffs she strives for greater resiliency building and more kid-centered activities within the classroom. With kids she strives to promote pro-social thoughtfulness and intergroup acceptance.

Michelle Karns has a bachelor's degree from Fort Wright College, and from Seattle University both a master's degree in public administration and a certificate in alcohol studies. She has worked as a therapist, a teacher, a trainer, and a writer. She currently resides in Davis, California, with her husband, Robert, and her daughter, Katy.

About National Training Associates

National Training Associates (NTA), founded in 1982, is a training and consultation firm comprised of specialists who serve as organizational and community catalysts. Staff members strive to facilitate processes that will contribute to success in the millennium.

NTA's goal is to encourage positive social change and build regional capacity through the development of local expertise and resident coaches. NTA does this through conferences, town meetings, presentations, workshops, seminars, and laboratories. The proposed task dictates the recommended delivery vehicle.

The services offered by NTA are best viewed from the perspective of how well they address the specific needs identified by a school, business, or community. Central to NTA's overall approach is the development and nourishment of teams and community partnerships.

Building Capacity

NTA employs the phrase "building capacity" to refer to the transformation taking place in all kinds of organizations. NTA's goal is to ensure local capacity rather than a dependency on imported expertise. Successful strategies have proven to be future-focused rather than problem-centered, proactive rather than reactive, and community based.

To achieve the building of capacity, a coaching component is included in all training and consultation services. Coaches become mentors to their colleagues, available to encourage and model the incorporation of new skills. This sustains enthusiasm for new learning and support for both personal and organizational change.

Co-sponsorship of Trainings and Conferences

For the past ten years, NTA has been working with state departments, county agencies, school districts, and community groups in all areas of the United States. Co-sponsored events are skill-oriented and highly individualized to meet presenting needs. While NTA trainers are often utilized, other resources are utilized as well.

A typical planning process includes the following steps:

- Collaborative assessment of needs
- Design of training/conference format and agenda
- Contractual agreements with speakers and trainers
- Marketing services and distribution of information through regional meetings, direct mail, and World Wide Web
- Preregistration
- On-site conference/training logistics

Consultation Services

NTA provides technical assistance in the areas of organizational planning, team building, productivity improvement, management training, and communication skill-building. The goal is to create site capability so that institutions can look within for future planning assistance rather than to outside experts. Most consultation assignments are facilitative in nature. Through interactive processes, the consultant helps organizations with the following tasks:

- Set the stage for systematic change by building group cohesion.
- Negotiate the steps toward an achievable, group-defined goal.
- Preview operational processes to maximize resources, define roles, and streamline procedures.
- Assess effectiveness through the use of feedback and realignment techniques.

Training and Consultation Topics

NTA's goal is to develop a positive culture that encourages and supports healthy choices. The areas of training and consultation are divided into *macro* (NTA facilitates the overall process) and *micro* (NTA focuses on various facilitation skills that lead to the success of specific programs). On both levels, facilitation skills become the foundation on which change is built.

At the *macro* level, NTA helps organizations create or enhance a comprehensive "living plan." This entails exploring and prioritizing belief systems, working to build unity, and developing a plan for the future through collaborative processes. NTA does this with school districts, communities, businesses, and administrative units. Those who participate leave with a personal commitment to change.

At the *micro* level, NTA teaches the skills and knowledge needed to implement a "living plan," with trainings focused on a specific set of requested techniques and strategies.

For a complete list of NTA's training topics, along with content descriptions and information about trainers, go to NTA Online, www.nta-yes.com.

Also Available from NTA

How to Create Positive Relationships with Students:
A Handbook of Group Activities and Teaching Strategies
by Michelle Karns

The innovative approach in this book provides communication skills for teachers and 50 easy-to-do activities designed to open communication windows. Each activity also provides students with experiences that will enable them to develop a repertoire of problem-solving strategies.
STOCK # 5032: $23.95

ProTactics: The Integration of Resiliency into the Classroom
by Michelle Karns

This one-hour videotape captures the essence of Michelle Karns and her driving passion to affect the way adults connect with kids. She challenges all educators to examine the present and work for an improved future.
STOCK # 5035: $39.95

The Power of Participation:
Improving Schools in a Democratic Society
by Dr. Raymond J. Golarz and Marion J. Golarz

The authors present the why (rationale, philosophy, and objectives) and the how (procedures for implementation and evaluation) of participatory governance. Their wisdom comes through clearly and their personal stories will help educators maintain a sense of perspective during the uncertain times of change.
STOCK # 5002: $19.95

NTA National Training Associates

P.O. Box 1270, Sebastopol, CA 95473   (800) 624-1120 PHONE
info@nta-yes.com EMAIL   www.nta-yes.com NTA ONLINE